The Magdalene Version:
Secret Wisdom from a Gnostic
Mystery School

Stuart Wilson and Joanna Prentis

PO Box 754, Huntsville, AR 72740

800-935-0045 or 479-738-2348; fax 479-738-2448

www.ozarkmt.com

© 2012 by Stuart Wilson and Joanna Prentis

All rights reserved. No part of this book, in part or in whole, may be reproduced, transmitted or utilized in any form or by any means, electronic, photographic or mechanical, including photocopying, recording, or by any information storage and retrieval system without permission in writing from Ozark Mountain Publishing, Inc. except for brief quotations embodied in literary articles and reviews.

For permission, serialization, condensation, adaptions, or for our catalog of other publications, write to Ozark Mountain Publishing, Inc., P.O. Box 754, Huntsville, AR 72740, ATTN: Permissions Department.

Library of Congress Cataloging-in-Publication Data
Wilson, Stuart, 1937 -
Prentis, Joanna, 1943 -
The Magdalene Version, by Stuart Wilson and Joanna Prentis
Here is the real voice of Mary Magdalene, giving secret teachings from her Mystery School!

1. Mary Magdalene 2. Women Disciples 3. Jeshua 4. Hypnosis
5. Metaphysics
I. Wilson, Stuart, 1937- II. Prentis, Joanna, 1943- III. Mary Magdalene
IV. Metaphysics IV. Title

Library of Congress Catalog Card Number: 2012941157
ISBN: 978-1-886940-29-1

Cover Art and Layout: www.noir33.com
Book set in: Times New Roman
Book Design: Julia Degan

Published by:

WWW.OZARKMT.COM
Printed in the United States of America

One Energy and Consciousness
in all that is
and all existence
as one Web of Life.

"The Way of Light"
quoted by Alariel in *Beyond Limitations.*

Contents

Part One:

Essenes and Gnostics

The teachings of Mary Magdalene
were the culmination
of the whole arc
of Essene and Gnostic development.

Alariel in Chapter 29

1. Alariel

We have been writing these books very much on the basis of our inner guidance and have learned to trust that guidance over the years. When Joanna and I were working on our first book, *The Essenes: Children of the Light,* we focused entirely on the past-life evidence, and although that evidence opened a window on the world in Israel 2,000 years ago, it did not give us access to all the information we wanted. Working within the framework of past-life research, there will always be areas which you cannot access simply because you are unable to find the right people in the right place at the right time. For example, it might seem to some people that anyone who had a life 2,000 years ago in Israel might be a useful source of information on the group around Jeshua, but a very conservative Pharisee living at that time may have regarded Jeshua as a dangerous radical who was undermining the Judaic tradition!

Note: We have used the name *Jeshua* throughout this book as it has not been proved that he was ever called "Jesus" during his own lifetime whereas the evidence for him being called Jeshua or Yeshua is substantial. We have also used BCE (Before the Common Era) and CE (Common Era) as being more universally acceptable than BC and AD.

When Joanna and I got as far as investigating past-life experiences in Atlantis, we were beginning to move into new and more challenging areas. Part of that research focused on my life as an architect on Atlantis called Anquel, and his story is told in depth in our book *Atlantis and the New Consciousness.* We were surprised and excited when our inner guidance told us that Anquel had found a most interesting source of information. This source would be difficult to access, and our best chance would be to ask Anquel a question *which we knew he would be unable to answer.*

This was an unusual piece of guidance, but we decided to follow it and starting casting about in our minds for a suitable question to ask. We already knew that Anquel had an interest in *a slow meditational form of movement,* and this sounded to us something like an Atlantean form of Tai Chi. Taking this as our starting point, we then constructed a question along the lines that our guidance had suggested and put this to Anquel.

Joanna: We are interested in the slow meditational form of movement that you mentioned. There is a group of people called the Essenes who live many thousands of years in the future from your time. We understand that the Essenes have a form of meditational movement and wonder if you could research this for us.

Anquel: I have never heard of these people, and if they exist in the future, I would have no way of researching this information by conventional means. However, I do have an angelic source who might be able to help. I will ask him to speak to you directly.

Comment by Stuart: There followed a long pause, and Joanna sensed that a different energy was starting to focus through me. Then the communication began again: *This is Alariel, speaking for a group of twelve angels who work with the Order of Melchizedek . . .*

Once the communication had been established, we were able to dialogue freely with Alariel although he made it clear that he was not an omniscient source—indeed, he denied the existence of such a source anywhere in the universe. He told us he had regular contact with archangels, and they worked closely with the Elohim, the highest level of Beings who could be regarded as personalized to even a tiny degree. Beyond the Elohim, he said there was only the totally transpersonal Energy and Consciousness of Father-Mother God. Even the Elohim, he told us, do not claim to be omniscient and for a very simple reason. In star systems where there is free will, the unexpected is always happening, and if you are unable to predict these outcomes, you cannot possibly be omniscient! Alariel told us that the very idea of omniscience is a strange and illogical human invention.

Alariel was also clear about the questions that he would not answer. When Joanna asked him about questions he might be forbidden to answer, this was his reply.

Alariel: There are some questions that we *choose* not to answer, and these come into three categories:

1. There are Words of Power which give access to control frequencies in the angelic world. We obviously would not reveal these.

2. There is information which forms part of the research which other groups on Earth are well advanced on, and will soon reveal: we would not wish to 'steal their thunder.'

3. And finally there are concepts so far beyond your present understanding that they would disorient you and cause you distress. It is not a kindness to reveal this type of information, and we will not do so.

Having said that, there is still a vast amount of information for you to explore.

We did not realize it at the time, but this last sentence understated the situation quite dramatically. When we went on later to ask Alariel one big question—*How do we create our own reality?*—a whole book emerged from that single question! (It was published as our third book, *Beyond Limitations: The Power of Conscious Co-Creation.*) However, even in our second book, *Power of the Magdalene,* Alariel's involvement changed and eventually entirely transformed our work. As we continued to explore this area, we discovered that many things were simply not clear to the people on the ground who were going through their lives in Israel from day to day.

For example, even if we had asked our main contact in our first book—the Essene elder Daniel Benezra—he might not have been able to give us the answers we wanted. If we had asked Daniel how many female disciples of Jeshua there were, he might simply not have known or might have answered, "Oh, many" or "Quite a few," and this would not have advanced our research very much. But when we asked Alariel about this, what we got was a precise answer that transformed our knowledge of discipleship at that time.

Alariel: It's important to understand that the discipleship system that Jeshua set up was designed to mirror the greater symbolism of the universe. The balance of Father-Mother God was mirrored in a balance of male and female disciples, so there were six circles of twelve, making seventy-two male disciples, and six circles of twelve, making seventy-two female disciples, a total of 144 disciples in all.

Comment by Stuart: Of course, Alariel did not stop there, and he gave us a vast amount of information on the female disciples, especially the first circle of twelve which contained some remarkably advanced Initiates like Mother Mary (Mary Anna) and Mary Magdalene.

Our relationship with Alariel changed and evolved over time, and gradually through this contact we came to see him as a channeling source of remarkable depth and clarity. Some of the information we received surprised us, and much of it stretched our imagination and challenged us to expand our awareness. Our dialogues with Alariel transformed our work, and his insight and knowledge gave our research a depth which a past-life process alone could not have provided. And these dialogues have taken us on a journey that has opened up a window onto a vital and fascinating time in history—a journey in which we now invite you to share.

2. The Essene and Gnostic Heritage

Despite a rapidly growing literature, the Gnostics remain strangely enigmatic. Though it is widely assumed that Gnosticism was an exclusively Christian movement, there is now mounting evidence that many of the most active Gnostic groups traced their origins back to much earlier roots. Some of the main strands of Gnostic thought can be found in Judaism before the birth of Jeshua, but other elements go back to Persian and Zoroastrian traditions—and perhaps even earlier to ancient Babylon. Far from being simply a heretical offshoot of Christianity, Gnosticism seems to be emerging as a quite separate movement with strong pre-Christian roots.

There is also a widely held view that Gnosticism was centralized. In fact, there was never a single, universally accepted and "orthodox" Gnosticism but a whole range of Gnostic possibilities. Some scholars (including J.J. Hurtak) talk of twenty or even thirty varieties of Gnostic belief. Some of these could be called sects while others focused around a single individual and his followers. It seems clear that there was a wide variety of Gnostic theory and practice. None of this added up to the existence of any kind of Gnostic

"Church," and, indeed, the whole concept of a Church would probably have been distasteful to the great majority of freethinking and independent Gnostics.

Many people also believe that Gnostic texts were unknown in the West prior to the discoveries at Nag Hammadi. In fact, Gnostic texts have long been known to scholars, and the discovery of the Nag Hammadi Library in Egypt in 1945 was only the culmination of a series of important discoveries. These include *Pistis Sophia,* part of the Askew Codex which was purchased by the British Museum in 1795; and *The Gospel of Thomas,* discovered in Egypt in 1898; the Bruce Codex, brought to England around 1769; and the Papyrus Berolinensis, acquired by a German scholar in Cairo in 1896. This last discovery is also called the Berlin Gnostic Codex or the Akhmim Codex and contains versions of the *Apocryphon of John,* the *Sophia of Jesus Christ,* and the *Gospel of Mary.*

For all the current interest in the Gnostic tradition and despite a plethora of books on this subject, the Gnostics remain shadowy and elusive. This is partly because they have been studied largely within a Christian rather than an Essene context. Yet the truth is that it is impossible to understand the Gnostic movement unless we start with the Essenes. Many of those who moved on to become Gnostics had originally come from Essene families, and even those who did not were influenced by many of the ideas in the Essene tradition, a subject we explored through past-life accounts in *The Essenes: Children of the Light* and *Power of the Magdalene.* That is why we are beginning this book with a reconnection with Essene lives. These experiences form a vital foundation for understanding the Gnostic impulse and putting it into perspective.

That context has resonances right up to the present day and can at times be both controversial and challenging. The more one examines the Essene-Gnostic connection, the more extensive and convincing this becomes. Some of the most powerful and far-reaching Gnostic concepts—such as the idea of God as both Father and Mother—are directly traceable to an Essene source. The combination of an Earthly Mother and a Heavenly Father was one of the central themes of the Essene tradition, and it occurs frequently in Essene texts. When one considers the links in both personnel and concepts that unite the Essenes and the Gnostics, one begins to see the Gnostics in a new way as the direct inheritors and continuers of the Essene tradition. One of the strengths of the Essene movement was its ability to draw from and absorb key elements in other wisdom traditions, including Pythagorean concepts, Egyptian Mystery School material, and Zoroastrianism. Hence, the existence of other non-Essene sources within the Gnostic movement is simply the continuation of a well-worn path of assimilation.

The more one considers the realities of the Essene-Gnostic line of development, the more absurd it becomes to see the Gnostics as a mere offshoot of Christianity. Of course, it would have been most convenient for the early Church Fathers to be able to dismiss the Gnostic movement as a misguided Christian heresy, but there is very little evidence to support this perception.

What emerges clearly from a study of this period is that there were, in fact, *two* main forms of Christianity: the highly structured, ritualistic, and doctrinal Church established by Peter and Paul and an alternative Gnostic form which was not a religion but a process and a fellowship of individuals following a spiritual path.

Of course, our attitudes are colored by the whole weight of history, and it might seem absurd even to question whether the form of Christianity which survived was the best one—or the one that leads to the greatest enlightenment and the highest level of spiritual development. However, recent developments within Christianity as a whole have now brought questions like these into a much sharper focus, and we now stand at a crossroads in the spiritual development of the West where the only way forward might be to consider a broader range of options. Many Christian churches are now perceived to be resistant to change and unsympathetic to the capacity for leadership now being shown by empowered women. In these circumstances it may be time to re-examine the Gnostic alternative to see if it offers a viable way forward in this modern age.

3. Yianna and the Essenes

Late in November 2007, Jaye Woodfield, a counselor living in Gloucestershire, came to see us to do a past-life session. Jaye already had a sense of connection with the time in Israel 2,000 years ago, and Joanna took her back to this period. After the usual induction sequence, this was how the session developed.

Joanna: Can you tell me what you are seeing, sensing, or hearing?

Jaye: I'm in a crowd of people. It's like a small market-place. Jeshua is standing on something to make him taller.

Joanna: So that he stands out from the crowd?

Jaye: Yes. There's a lot of noise, a lot of commotion, and he can't be heard. I'm standing at the edge of the crowd and just watching the whole scene.

Joanna: Can you hear what he's saying?

Jaye: The words are lost . . . I think people are mocking him.

Joanna: How does that make you feel?

Jaye: Really helpless. I want to help him, but I can't get near. There are just people shouting—shouting at each other and shouting at him. There's just complete turmoil. And I can see big rough men in armor. I think they're Romans . . . they're so big and brutal and angry. And they're taking him, just dragging him now.

Joanna: So they've dragged him away?

Jaye: Well, he's just disappeared . . . I can't see.

Joanna: And no one is telling you what's happened?

Jaye: No. I feel sick . . .

Joanna: Are you fearing for his life?

Jaye: I just feel that he's very vulnerable, and no one wants to help him. I want to help . . . I'm quite alone; there's no one else I know here. I'm just having to watch it really. I don't know where they've gone . . .

Joanna: Are you a woman?

Jaye: Yes, I am . . . I'm shy. I've got something covering my face. I'm wearing a sort of head-dress. It's blue, and I've put half of it over my face because I don't want to be seen . . .

Comment by Stuart: Later on during this session we established that her name was Yianna, so we'll use that name from this point on. The session with Jaye continues.

Joanna: So this meeting where Jeshua was, did you go to give him support, or did you want to hear him talk?

Yianna: Yes, I wanted to hear him talk. It's a meeting place, but there are no stalls. It's not a market.

Joanna: Was Jeshua a teacher for you?

Yianna: I think he's someone I've been drawn to. This image came strongly, this busy place with lots of noise . . .

Joanna: It sounds as if you're used to quieter places.

Yianna: Yes, I' m very quiet . . . I'm in a dimly lit room with a candle and an arch and a window . . .

Joanna: *Is there a nice feeling of tranquility?*

Yianna: Yes, it's very simple, very humble. I think I'm about eighteen, but there are younger children around me . . .

Joanna: *Are these your brothers and sisters?*

Yianna: Yes, I think they're brothers and sisters. But there's such peace. Everybody is just busy and peaceful. It's just simplicity . . .

Joanna: *So is your job to help your mother in the house?*

Yianna: I don't get any sense of my parents at all . . . I think I'm to be married . . . but I don't want to be married to him.

Joanna: *Why? Don't you like him very much?*

Yianna: He's not the one for me . . . it's like an arranged marriage . . . it's something I have to do. I feel a sense of loyalty and duty. I think he's someone who works at the court . . . it's somewhere I don't want to be. My heart is here in this simplicity . . .

Joanna: *So you see yourself going from a simple life to something quite different?*

Yianna: Yes . . . I've got a picture of him now. He's short and dark, and he's a very kind man. I'm very vulnerable. I'm very shy, and I can see it's a good idea to marry him. I don't know what it will bring - I'm very confused.

Joanna: *What kind of work does he do?*

Yianna: He's an official at Herod's court, and he's a Pharisee.

Comment by Stuart: The Pharisees were the rabbinic group which controlled the educational system operating through the synagogues. When the Sadducees and the Essenes disappeared, the Pharisaic group was left as the mainstream of modern Judaism.

The session with Yianna continues.

Joanna: Can you tell me about King Herod's court?
Yianna: It's too much. It's not the place for me.
Joanna: Too many people, too much noise?
Yianna: It's wrong, the wrong environment . . . I want to marry in order to spread some goodness there, to bring something to it . . . The court's very vivid . . . I'm experiencing a lot. I seem to be there now.
Joanna: Are you married now?
Yianna: Yes. There are terrible things, too much color . . . it's a vile place. I can't bear it . . . I'm not happy . . . There's a big rift between me and my husband . . . There's a lot of bullying; everybody's bullying someone. The court is just a place of bullies, so I'm drawn to escaping to a gentle community of people. I think it must be the Essenes. This is a group that I resonate with . . .
Joanna: So what was memorable about the Essenes?
Yianna: Healing. I needed to be healed so many times because of everything upsetting me so much. I need to go there and be quiet . . . I just wanted to be with them more and more.
Joanna: Did you wish to learn how to be a healer yourself?

Yianna: Yes.

Joanna: *So were they able to show you how to heal?*

Yianna: I think it's just being with them . . . their resonance and their wisdom.

Joanna: *Did they accept people from outside their community?*

Yianna: I gave them money . . . I was wealthy. It was a very quiet place where Jeshua would come and the disciples, too. They looked very tired and disheveled and needed food . . . I wanted to be there when they came. I think this was more to escape from the court although I did help with the cooking. We were making lots of food . . .

Joanna: *Did you feel there was equality between the men and the women?*

Yianna: It was all very easy. It was like no other place.

Joanna: *Would the difference between the court of Herod and the Essenes be that you felt respected as a woman with the Essenes but not at the court?*

Yianna: Yes. I felt at home with the Essenes, but I was helping, too, and it was important for me to contribute. And just to be in their company was healing.

Joanna: *Did you remember any particular event when you were with the Essenes?*

Yianna: There was a lot of jesting going on. It was very light-hearted. I don't remember Jeshua really preaching . . .

Joanna: *Maybe he didn't have to. Maybe you learned from his energy . . .*

Yianna: He was full of fun. He was just such fun.

Joanna: *What other memories do you have of him?*

Yianna: A lovely gentleness, really lovely. He was

very warm . . . there was such familiarity. There were jokes about where they were going to go next:

'We've been there.'

'No, we haven't been there.'

'We need to go there.'

'Oh, I don't want to go there.'

(At this point Jaye chuckled.)

I'm sitting and mending some sandals. I remember stitching the leather soles. It's great to be here.

Joanna: *And Mary Magdalene?*

Yianna: Ah, Mary Magdalene: very special, quite awesome, and fiery. With long hair. As you would say, 'They are together.'

Joanna: *You know that because of the energy or because it was common knowledge in your group?*

Yianna: No, the energy between them. She's very graceful and tends to him beautifully. The connection is lovely, and she's beautiful but quite commanding.

Joanna: *Beautiful in the sense that she has an inner beauty?*

Yianna: Long wavy hair and she wears white . . . The disciples wore brown clothes really more like sacking.

Joanna: *What about the female disciples?*

Yianna: I can only see Mary at the moment in this scene where I'm sitting mending the sandals. Mary is sitting next to him, and there's light-hearted banter going on. She's putting a hand on his shoulder and saying he needs to rest. And he is saying, 'What? Rest, woman? Me?'

Joanna: *Jeshua had so much to do . . .*

18

Yianna: I think he had been on some mission, and we had been cooking for their return.

Joanna: *Well, everyone had their work to do, but everyone was honored for the work they did because together they made a team.*

Yianna: Yes. These are definite scenes, but I can't seem to move on from them. The quiet room, very simple in ocher-like colors, and the court scene with a big table, lavish, horrible, too much color, too much finery. It makes me shiver and shake to think of it . . . I don't really see my husband. I remember him being short and stocky.

Joanna: *What did he think about your trips to the Essene community?*

Yianna: I think it caused a rift between us. He wanted me to enjoy the court life. There were lots of women for me there and a comfortable lifestyle. I think he had a senior position . . . He was kind to me . . . but he didn't want me to be associated with Jeshua. He was embarrassed.

Joanna: *Was your husband anxious in case your mixing with Jeshua and his disciples might threaten his job at court?*

Yianna: Yes. I remember the court very well: the steps, the fire, the doors, the noise—dreadful, dreadful. And the high table—dancing—a very colorful place. Wine, too much, everything, too much . . .

Joanna: *So the people at court were out of control with alcohol while the Essenes had a quieter kind of joy?*

Yianna: They had such purity and simplicity—it was where I wanted to be.

Joanna: *Do you recall Mother Mary?*

Yianna: I don't remember her. It's only Mary Magdalene . . . I see her face . . . we became friends. She was asking me a lot about the court. She's quite fascinated by it, and a bit in awe of it. This was obviously a side of me she was intrigued by because I was there. It was supposedly my home, but I used to spend more and more time away from it.

Joanna: *Did this ever cause a scene between you and your husband?*

Yianna: There's one incident where he sent a party out to get me back, and they're dragging me back. He's being very brutal. He says he's had enough.

Joanna: *What's the next important event which happens in your life?*

Yianna: Being with the community. We're preparing for something. There's unrest, and we're confused. It's unusual because we're so peaceful. We're anxious but we shouldn't be.

Joanna: *Has something happened to Jeshua?*

Yianna: Something's about to. We're trying to prepare for it not being all right . . . We can't believe it. We don't want to lose this site.

Joanna: *Go forward now to see what has happened. You were with a crowd jostling, and he was taken away. What happened after that?*

Yianna: I go back and tell the others because they weren't there. Mary wants to know. She's very upset. I stay with her, trying to comfort her. She's distraught, and there's a lot of elders around . . . I just remember that scene, not believing and not wanting to know . . . I want to stay with it and see. I keep trying to find out what's happening . . . Now I'm getting a vision of the cross, which is difficult to look at, but I'm there.

Joanna: Are the other disciples?

Yianna: The women. Mary's with me. She's looking different; she's looking older. She's wearing different clothes; she's wearing something that is so dark brown it's almost black. She's distraught, very faint, very quiet. She doesn't want to stay.

Joanna: I don't suppose you do either . . .

Yianna: No, but I do.

Joanna: What happened next?

Yianna: He's being taken down. Mary's not there. I think it's my job to report. Yes . . . it's leading up a track with bushes. I'm not allowed to go on. There are people on guard. I don't feel sad now. I just need to know what's happening. It's my duty to inform. I just want to know what's happening—that feeling has taken over . . .

Joanna: Do you know what happened with his body?

Yianna: I've been following them, but I can't go any further. It's like a garden with bushes, including myrtle. There's dense vegetation and the tomb—yes, I know it. I can see it. The white cave . . . I'm seeing it now, but I wasn't allowed to follow. It was my duty to tell Mary Magdalene what had happened. I'm spending time with her, reassuring her.

Joanna: So do you have an intuitive feeling that Jeshua is all right?

Yianna: Yes, I do . . . I'm getting an image of him lying in this cave on the right hand side of it quite near the entrance. And there are people tending him in quite a frantic way . . . the cave is full of smells, herbs, but I don't know what herbs they are . . . Why I'm seeing inside the tomb I don't know, but it's a strong vision I have...He's sitting on the stone bench, looking fragile and worn out, and I ask what I can do. I say, 'Master, what can I do?' And he says, 'Go and get Mary.' And that's what I do. I run and run. I go and fetch her, and she comes back with me . . .

At this point Jaye broke off her account and asked a searching question:

Is this normal, when you can only remember bits and these bits fade?

Joanna: Yes, I know. I understand.

Yianna: Because it's so frustrating . . .

Joanna: But it was extremely emotional for you . . .

Yianna: I was panicking . . . it's so frustrating . . . I've only got these images, and nothing seems to be continuous . . .

Joanna: That's like far memory: you remember bits, but sometimes you don't remember the bits in between . . . What happens when you get to the tomb with Mary?

Yianna: We both go in, and I come out, because I don't want to be there when she sees him because it's very special, and their relationship is very special, and I don't feel right to be there, so I go out. I don't know what to do . . . I want to tell everybody, and yet I'm not allowed to.

Joanna: Had you been sworn to secrecy?

Yianna: Yes—and yet it's an overwhelming need . . .

Joanna: Yes, because he's all right. He's not dead.

22

Yianna: But there's a lot of confusion afterwards because for most people, it got out that he had died. It had to be like that, or otherwise he couldn't have gone on to do his later work. Obviously, you would want to tell people that he lived, but you mustn't tell them . . .

Joanna: *So you've left Mary, what happens next?*

Yianna: I don't go to the court any more. I'm very aware that the community is home. That's where I go . . . I just want to live with them in a quiet way, and I give them the news. I'm there to tell them that . . .

Joanna: *Was it just a small number of people you were allowed to tell that to?*

Yianna: Yes, I am to keep it quiet . . . this is why I am so quiet now . . . it's as if I have knowledge, but I can't tell anyone. That's why I never speak up. It's had a profound effect—so now I know.

Joanna: *And was there was a lot of confusion afterwards?*

Yianna: I knew when he was taken down so quickly this might mean that he wasn't dead . . .

Joanna: *About that time there was a lot of unrest, a lot of trouble with the Romans . . .*

Yianna: I think I became quite reclusive . . . I stayed with the community. I see myself as just being quiet and doing simple tasks . . . I became almost like a nun. I stayed with the community, not wanting to go anywhere. I think I felt very much a part of it . . . I needed to recover . . . It was a big strain, and my husband had abandoned me.

Joanna: *After Mary left Israel, did you ever see her*

again?

Yianna: I don't think I did.

Joanna: *She had to leave Israel, so if you had elected to stay, you wouldn't have seen her again.*

Yianna: I stayed with the Essene community and became very much part of it . . . I'm looked after . . . (At this point there was deep emotion, sobbing, and a sense of emotional release.)

Joanna: *The communities were able to continue for a time, but many of the disciples were going their different ways. Did you ever meet the disciple Luke, who was healing in the tomb?*

Yianna: Yes, he was the one whose sandals I was mending.

Joanna: *Luke was quite a character, but he was a great healer.*

Yianna: Yes, he was lovely. Yes.

Comment by Stuart: Luke's account is given in our first book, *The Essenes: Children of the Light*.

The session with Yianna continues.

Joanna: *When you reached the end of that incarnation and looked back at the whole of your life, what was the main lesson learned from that life?*

Yianna: I had done what I was supposed to do. I was a part of it. I think I wondered if I could have done more. Perhaps I should have done more . . . I remember the days before the crucifixion were just blissful . . .

Joanna: *Just being in Jeshua's presence . . .*

Yianna: Yes, it was bliss.

We asked Alariel to comment on this session, and this was what he said.

Alariel: A most interesting life because Yianna bridged two quite different parts of Jewish society: the largely Pharisaic group at the court and the quieter and more spiritual group of Essenes in the community. One of the weaknesses of the Essenes was their tendency to become isolated from the rest of the Jews, who were following a very different path. Because of this, they valued any input they could get from the wider context of Judaism, and being able to access information on court life would have been quite valuable to them.

Comment by Stuart: It also seems clear that Yianna's main reason for being at court was to provide financial assistance to support Jeshua and the disciples, and although she found court life distasteful, this role did prove important to the Ministry.

4. Lyn

In August 2008, our friend Lyn came to do a past-life session. She has been trained in Quantum Healing Hypnosis Therapy by Dolores Cannon, and she practices a number of healing modalities. Lyn is also a talented artist. She wanted to focus on any life experience she may have had 2,000 years ago in Israel, and this is how the session began.

Joanna: If you could tell me what you're sensing, seeing, or hearing.

Lyn: It looks like a sunlit village . . . lots of square walls and stonework . . . And there's a courtyard in the middle . . . a lot of animals around.

Joanna: Do you have a sense of the temperature?

Lyn: Hot.

Joanna: And can you see any people?

Lyn: I can see one person: a boy with dark hair . . . he's nine or ten, I think. He's waiting for something. The people have gone off for some kind of gathering, and he's waiting for them to come back.

Joanna: Has the boy done much traveling himself?

Lyn: Not very much . . . now I can see people coming back with wares and rugs.

Joanna: Can he tell you about any of the people who

27

come back?

Lyn: There's someone called Elijah . . . he's very interested in circulating the knowledge they receive when they go off on their travels.

Joanna: Who amongst this group has the most importance? Is it Elijah?

Lyn: Yes.

Joanna: So is Elijah the head of the village?

Lyn: Yes.

Joanna: And they do a lot of travelling . . .

Lyn: . . . and they trade.

Comment by Stuart: Lyn talked about a trip to Damascus, something that excited the boy, and this is where we pick up the account again.

Joanna: So would the boy go forward and take us on this trip to Damascus? We can go straight there. Could the boy tell us what happens next?

Lyn: It's like a cobbled street, but there are huge stones . . . there's a market . . . white walls . . . then there's a circle of people with Jeshua.

Joanna: What is the boy's first impression of Jeshua?

Lyn: He feels the energy.

Joanna: Is this the first time the boy has seen Jeshua?

Lyn: He's heard about him . . .

Joanna: And when the boy sees Jeshua, how does he react?

Lyn: Very emotionally, very overwhelmed, very impassioned, totally in awe and filled with total love.

Joanna: *While he's in Damascus, does he see Jeshua many times?*

Lyn: There's a really strong connection between this group and Jeshua, like a kindred feeling in the work they're doing. He wants to see the boy again, and there are some initiations he can do with Jeshua, including developing his gifts. There are lots of colors here—turquoise, blues, whites, reds, oranges. And the boy is just so pleased to see everybody. They all know they've got to keep going, spreading the knowledge.

Joanna: *Does the boy want to talk about the person he became when he grew up?*

Lyn: He's just giving a blessing . . . the other children have taken to him and he's very pleased to be in the process . . . There was a ceremony with oils, with water, with hands and with prayers . . . It was an inclusion, the opening of a pathway, an initiation on the path of knowledge, and there will be other initiations as he grows up, but this key experience of meeting Jeshua has given him something that he will follow.

Joanna: *Where does the boy want to take us next?*

Lyn: I think there's a woman in pale blue, very pretty . . . I think her name is Anne.

Joanna: *Is she part of this group of people?*

Lyn: Yes, she is . . . Anne is very much involved in herbs and oils. She's blended these oils, and she provides them for all the initiations. She has much wisdom . . . she has been to Egypt.

Comment by Stuart: At this point we established that her full name was Mary Anne, so we will use that form of the name from now on.

The session with Lyn continues.

Joanna: Where would the boy like to go next?
Lyn: We're in Jerusalem . . .
Joanna: What age is he now?
Lyn: He's about twenty now.
Joanna: What brings him to Jerusalem?
Lyn: Jeshua.
Joanna: And what is he going to do in Jerusalem?
Lyn: He's going to work with Mary Anne and develop the oils and restore the health of Jeshua . . . There are plans that have been made, and he's helping to support the process . . . It all has to be kept very quiet.
Joanna: Yes. So what's your understanding of the situation?
Lyn: We will nurture Jeshua . . . and we'll help Jeshua to come through . . . the oil is very potent . . . It's a very ancient mixture from the ancient temples. Mary Anne has been working on this . . .
Joanna: So as a man, you are well-versed in the use of oils for healing?
Lyn: Yes, I'm more detached than Mary Anne and focused on the gifts and the blessings. There's a group of people who will be doing the anointing of the oil and another group will be saying the prayers.
Joanna: Is Mary Anne directing the group using the oils?
Lyn: Yes.

Joanna: *Would you like to tell us about what happened during this process?*

Lyn: The whole group is being affected by fear—we're in fear of our lives . . . We're just waiting for the moment when Jeshua arrives . . . he's being brought down to the cave—he's come down from the cross . . . The fear in my stomach beforehand was just incredible . . .

Joanna: *So it's a key role that you feel a lot of responsibility about?*

Lyn: Yes—a great privilege.

Joanna: *So were you one of the ones who prepared the oils?*

Lyn: Mary Anne prepared the oils, but they were anointed by me . . . The initiations helped to apply the gift of healing . . . I think Jeshua knew that those hands would be the ones that helped to revive him . . . The oils contained rose and other secret ingredients.

Joanna: *For you to have the job of applying the oils, you must have been very close to Jeshua. Were you?*

Lyn: Ever since the first meeting, a great bond.

Comment by Stuart: Even at this point we were unsure of the identity of Mary Anne, but Lyn went on to make it clear that she was Mary Magdalene. This explains the earlier statement that he was "more detached" than Mary Anne—who as the spiritual partner of Jeshua would obviously find it very difficult to be completely detached at this difficult time.

The session with Lyn continues.

Joanna: *Presumably there is still a certain amount of fear, but you're absorbed in the process?*

Lyn: Yes, we're just doing the work...it was such a gift, a privilege to be able to work like that, and I felt very grateful to all the elders who trained me and developed this work. We know we have done as much as we can.

Joanna: *After you've been in the tomb, what happens to you?*

Lyn: I have to remove all the things and leave Jerusalem . . . Mary Anne would be more involved in what happened then.

Joanna: *So what happened to you afterwards?*

Lyn: It feels very chaotic. I'm not sure about what's happening, and the knowledge of it was dangerous, too. I think I have to disappear.

Joanna: *Did you go back to your community?*

Lyn: Yes, with the news that things had gone better than we thought.

Joanna: *So there was a sadness in the parting, but also a satisfaction that you had played your part?*

Lyn: I now understand why I have had such colossal feelings of fear and have had to overcome them.

Joanna: *Did you manage to live to an old age?*

Lyn: I see an elderly being, but not being able to trust . . .

Joanna: *Is there anything else you need to know from that life?*

Lyn: Only the acknowledgment of the healing

work and the power of spirit and that the knowledge needs to be shared.

Comment by Stuart: This had been a remarkable session with Lyn—full of high energy and the sense of great heart quality and dedication. It took a long time for the identity of the person referred to at first simply as "Anne" to emerge, but when we realized that this was, in fact, Mary Magdalene, the whole story moved onto another level.

We knew from our earlier research that it was traditional in that culture to give a baby at least two (and sometimes even three) names and that they could also be identified by their place of origin—hence, Mary of Bethany and Joseph of Arimathea. We had never known Mary Magdalene's second name, but now we know that it was Anne. In the light of our knowledge of Mary's training in the Isis Temple in Alexandria (which emerged from our second book, *Power of the Magdalene*), it makes perfect sense that Mary Magdalene would be an expert on oils and be responsible for the preparation of the oils used in the healing process in the tomb.

Thanks to Lyn's experience, we now have another account of that healing process to lay alongside Daniel's chapter called "The Empty Tomb" in *The Essenes: Children of the Light* and Laura Clare's account in *Power of the Magdalene*. All these three accounts are very different: Daniel's overview was seen as an observer from the Interlife and the other two accounts were those of eyewitnesses who were there in the tomb at the time. They tell quite different stories because their focus was different, but taken together they give an in-depth account of the whole process of healing

Jeshua in the tomb. Yianna's account also gives confirmation of the healing process, but hers was seen as a vision rather than an eyewitness experience.

What is remarkable about these four accounts is not the differences in detail and perspective—which are totally understandable—but the confirmation of the healing process as a whole. The tasks involved and the perspectives differ, but the main outlines of this process come through with great clarity, and it all adds up to powerful corroboration of the main narrative of Jeshua's survival.

5. Sara and the Crystal

In November 2009, Pam came to visit us. Pam is a past-life therapist, and she worked with Vicky Wall, the originator of the Aura Soma color healing system. She wanted to focus on a life in Israel at the time of Jeshua, and we pick up the narrative when her life is just about to begin.

Pam: I'm in the Light, and I'm looking at things in the Light. Where I am is the one point of Light. I'm within the Oneness . . . From the point of Oneness, I'm going right back to my birth . . . So I'm just at the point of Light, and I'm looking forward to being born. I'm really excited about being born because I know this is going to be a very important life . . . I'm really excited, and I feel that I have the power and the Light that I need to come to do the work that I'm destined to do; I feel a tingle, and I feel excited about it, and I'm looking forward to being born. And I know that I'm going to be a female . . .

Joanna: *Do you remember your name?*

(After a little difficulty in focusing on the name, Pam said she had a big reaction to the name "Sara," so we'll use that name from this point on.)

Sara: Now it's as if time is slowing down, and it's beginning to feel very heavy. It's the heaviness of the dimension I'm coming into. I'm feeling the heaviness, but I'm all right with it. I've been prepared for this. I knew it would be heavy, but experience is never quite the same . . . and as I come in, it's like I've been born but I've not been born yet.

Joanna: *Do you feel that your body has been born, but your soul has not connected up with it yet?*

Sara: So I've been born, but I've not been born, and I'm coming into the body that's destined to be mine. I'm just wriggling into it, and it wriggles, and I'm quite happy with it, and I'm quite content, and I'm looking up at my mother and my father, and they're together, and they're looking at me, and there are a lot of other people around, and, yes, we are a community.

There's someone singing a song, a song that I remember. It's a song of welcome, but within that song there are harmonies within harmonies and words within words. The song is everything. The song is keying me in to pick up all the information I need to follow my destiny . . . I love the song.

So I have some brothers and sisters, and I grow up as a placid child . . . I'm very close to Jeshua in many ways . . . there was always Light around him and sparkles . . . I'm a child and I'm just playing in the dirt, and he's put me on his knee to show me something—a hen's feather . . .

Joanna: He was very good with children . . .

Sara: I felt very safe with him . . . from being small, I was close to him; from the time I was very young . . . I see my mother in that life . . . she had a way with the animals . . . she looked after the animals, she talked to them, and they spoke to her. The donkey that he rode into Jerusalem was found by her, and she felt pleased that he was riding her donkey. She was so full of wonder and love that he was riding her donkey, and that donkey had been well prepared, I tell you! (She laughs.)

          As I grew up, Jeshua would take time out to help me with whatever I was studying . . . there were eight children, and I was number two. In the beginning I was a precocious little madam, and then I settled down and I took my studies very seriously.

Joanna: Where did you go to study?

Sara: I studied at Mount Carmel, and some of the time we were in caves there.

Stuart: The community at Mount Carmel was built into the rock to some extent.

The session with Sara continues:

Sara: And Mother Mary was there sometimes. I was always a little bit in awe of her . . .

          I always had an interest in the crystals . . . I'm being shown a jewel. It's pink and Jeshua has given me the jewel, this crystal. It's a crystal that he found on his travels . . . he carried it with him everywhere he went after he found it until he put it into my hand.

Comment by Stuart: It was only after the session was over that we began to consider which Sara was involved here, bearing in mind that the name Sara was used by many families in Israel at that time. It's clear that Jeshua was always around—perhaps as an older child—while Sara was growing up, and this and the closeness of the connection suggests that they might have been related. In these circumstances, the most likely candidate seems to be the daughter of Mary Anna's brother, Isaac. That would make Sara and Jeshua cousins. We already knew that when this Sara grew up, she became one of the female disciples—see Chapter 9 of *Power of the Magdalene*.

The session with Sara continues.

Sara: We have to move on. We have to move forward to when there are dark clouds gathering, and I'm beginning to feel tense. It's as if for me everything's gone quiet, and I can't hear my song any more . . .

Joanna: *So if this is the time of the crucifixion, are you in your teens then or a bit older?*

Sara: A bit older . . . I can't sing my song anymore because I'm sad . . . the human part of me feels the sadness and the grief, but I have a job to do when I stand at the foot of the cross, holding this jewel, this crystal . . .

     I saw his face with the crown of thorns . . . I was fairly close so that I had to look up at him and put my head back. I wanted to be as close as I could even though I felt it might have been safer to be farther away, but I just had to be close . . . I just needed to look on his face until the end. I looked at his face all the time. People spoke to me, and I spoke to them, but I never took my eyes off his face because I couldn't bear to lose him . . .

He knew it was a crystal that he would need, and someone would need to hold it for him and have it close to him. I had to smuggle it in. No one must see it, and no one must know that I have the crystal. And although I have my sadness, my grief, my fears, my bewilderment, I'm very focused on the job in hand as he knew I would be, and this was the role I needed to play. This crystal reaches out. It reaches out far and wide into other crystals and all the places he has visited. It reaches into the depth of the Earth. It reaches into the heavens—it's a very special crystal. This crystal embodies the Light; it embodies all that he is.

My work is done. The crystal has exploded into Light. The pink is the Love, of course, the one heart. He says that's who I am, the one heart. And in the community I was the one heart. I held the Love and anchored it, the Love of the one heart, the Love of God. He called me "the one heart" . . . my heart and his and the one heart are joined together, and that's a celebration because from that, there is a new energy which encompasses the world that the world needed, and I cry the tears of the world. That's what I need to let go of.

He looked at me, and I felt I didn't quite look at him. I felt unworthy, and he tells me "No," and I was not and am not ... I have connected now . . . and it's almost as if part of me is raised up into the Light. There are many beings of Light here. He's holding me and many others. He's hugging each of us in turn, and then he says, "You must return" . . . But that was my job: to hold the crystal, to be the one heart, and to anchor that . . . And I haven't let go of it, and that's what they want to celebrate. I stayed at my post even in the dark times . . .

There's something more I have to do. There's someone standing there to my left. There's shining, Light shines from there, and it's a soldier, but he has the Light, and he's moved towards me. The human part of me is a little afraid because of the crystal, and the crystal must be kept safe.

Joanna: *And he's a Roman?*

Sara: He's a Roman. The crystal has been kept safe, and it's still there, and that's why he's walking towards me because what's in my heart is pulling him, magnetizing him, and he's holding me by the shoulders. He's looking into my eyes, and the human part of me is afraid, but the other part is just allowing him, and then he's walked off.

And that's what they're telling me to remember because if I felt some guilt, they're saying, 'You imagined this, and you needed to know that you fulfilled your mission then, and you are fulfilling it now.'

And Jeshua's saying, 'Thank you' for my role, and he's getting me to look into his eyes because what he wanted me to see was that there's no difference between him and me, and I couldn't take that on at the time, and he's saying, 'Do you understand it now?   Do you see it now?'

'Yes!'

So he wants to show me all that he saw—and he saw you and you!

Joanna: *I was very blessed then . . .*

Sara: I saw the Light in someone who was very dark and knew it was in everybody, and he says, 'That was my secret.'

And he says, 'This is what you do, and you have to believe it now.'

They have taken him down, and as I walked away, the crystal felt heavy—and yet at the same time, I felt incredibly light, and I have to do something now with the crystal, and I can take a few moments to prepare myself.   It's as if parts of the crystal are going into all parts of everywhere: not just the Earth, not just the universe but everything . . . and the crystal is made up of many jewel-like parts.   This lovely pale pink and these parts are going into all the universes because they have this cone-shaped part that is missing, so the crystal parts are going to fill these gaps, and they're going everywhere . . .

What's the thing you've wanted most of all . . . to be one with God, and they say that's your desire and that's your fulfillment, and now these crystals have been passed on. Oh! Everything has shifted!

I'm being brought back to the cross again. After they had taken him away and everyone had gone, I came back and was going to put the crystal at the foot of the cross, but I realized that wasn't the right thing to do, so I went back to go on with everything . . . If I look back, I don't see darkness any more. I see Light as if something's shifted, something's cleared; there is still darkness around, but I don't see it . . .

I'm no longer afraid . . . we're getting on a boat . . . I have to leave so much behind, and there's a storm . . . I don't really know where we're going . . .

Joanna: *Were there any Marys on the boat?*

Sara: Yes . . . It was a small boat and it was crowded!

Joanna: *Was it a good passage?*

Sara: It was a terrible passage!

Joanna: *And were you one of the ones who had to leave?*

Sara: It wasn't safe to stay. They knew that I was connected, that I was close . . . We're on this boat and we land, and it's almost as if we know this is the right place, and there is Joseph . . . We felt full of optimism and that we could start anew, but it was also strange . . . and again it was due to this crystal I was carrying. Again, people react in different ways to it . . . and it's the love energy, but some people here didn't want it . . .

There were times when I split off from the main group and went traveling, and I would sit and meditate, and away from the group, there wasn't that sustaining group energy and the love that was within the group . . . I was tuning into an energy that had been there since the very beginning, not the land itself but the place on the Earth where the land developed, and I just used to go and heal it.

Joanna: *Perhaps you needed to go because you had specialized work to do because of your understanding of the earth energies.*

Sara: Yes. And it was an earth energy which has been there almost since the beginning of time . . .

Joanna: *Did you ever get to hear what happened to Jeshua?*

Sara: I don't think so. There were all kinds of rumors, all kinds of stories, but if I tune in to my heart and to the crystal, I know that he was safe, but I don't know on what level. I know he was safe and that we never really left each other . . . And there's a big sigh: I wish it could have been different because it could have been.

Joanna: *It could have been, but people weren't ready?*

Sara: They weren't ready, no . . .

Joanna: *At the end of your life, did you make any vows?*

Sara: No. I just felt with this crystal and the one heart and the connection, it's complete within itself . . . But there's something more. As I died, I rose up and was able to see more than I had seen before, and I was with him, and he took me by the hand, and I looked, and there was bright Light everywhere around the land, and that puzzled me because it hadn't felt always that bright. There was a Light all around and although the Light couldn't be brought in because the people blocked it, the Light was close and there were shards of Light going into people.

When Jeshua was on the cross when I was linking in with the crystal, if I had looked into his eyes, it would have helped me . . . He did need the energy of the crystal and for me to be standing in exactly that spot, and there was a flash of Light between him and the crystal, and that was what he needed. It was like an opening, and there was the Light and this crystalline structure . . . And I'm seeing now what I would have seen if I had looked into his eyes, and it's like the most wonderful explosion of Light, and yet at the same time, it was utter peace and utter stillness. And he wants me to go through that with him now.

I just have to keep looking into his eyes. And I'm still looking into his eyes, and my vision is changing as it does when you look into another dimension, and so I'm seeing his eyes but I'm also looking beyond, and I'm just told to keep looking...It's as if he's switched on a switch, and for me it wasn't fireworks. It was just peace and calm, and that's what he wanted to give me then, but I was afraid to look into his eyes—not afraid exactly but I felt too humble, and if I had done as I have done now, it would have been much easier for me because that's how it was for him wherever he went.

There was a kind of everything to it that he wanted to give me, which I had in my heart and in the one heart, but it's now going into every aspect of my being: all my soul aspects, every part of me. And he says it's done, and that's why I came here today, so thank you, both of you for being here, and that's cleared the problem with my throat because I cough and splutter all the time, and if I'd looked into his eyes, my word would have been 'Love' because Love just is. There's no me, no you.

And now I'm more complete to perform my task that I need to do, and I'll remember this moment, and it will infiltrate into every part of my being from alpha to omega, and I'll be where I've wanted to be always: one with the Source until whatever comes next . . . thank you.

Comment by Stuart: This was a very moving session with high energy, and the depth of Sara's connection with Jeshua comes through like a shining thread, linking the whole narrative together. When she said, "There was a kind of everything to it that he wanted to give me," I found that very significant. According to one of the Gnostic Gospels, *The Dialogue of the Savior*, Mary Magdalene was described as "A woman who understands the All."

We were already aware from the past-life work described in *The Essenes: Children of the Light* that Jeshua was supported during the crucifixion on two levels: energy transmitted through an elaborate earth-energy system and energy generated by meditation in the Essene communities. Sara's account focusing on the importance of the crystal shows that this provided a third level of support. Holding such a powerful crystal would have been so vital a task that it is quite logical for Jeshua to entrust this to someone very close to him—a cousin who was also one of the first circle of female disciples.

6. The Essene Healing Skills
Perfected by Jeshua

The Essenes were also known throughout Israel as "the Therapeutae"—the Healers—and we wanted to follow up this area of research into the time of Jeshua. When we asked Alariel about this, we received this reply.

Alariel: There is a lot of confusion over the healing skills of the Essenes. Some people think, for example, that all Essenes were capable of miraculous healings whilst, in fact, only a few people, such as Jeshua, could work at this level. Daniel Benezra gave a very thorough summary of Essene healing skills, and this would make a good starting point.

Comment by Stuart: The passage which Alariel is referring to comes in Chapter 11 of our first book, *The Essenes: Children of the Light.*

Daniel: We saw healing as being on many levels. Of course, there are well-established methods, many of these using herbs, ointments, clay and crystals, but on the highest level we saw healing as a re-attunement to the essential note of the individual. In many cases, illness is the result of a discord which has been set up within the being of the sick person, so that the individual is like a musical instrument which has gotten out of tune. If the healer can work with the healing angels, they can assist in re-attuning the individual to his/her note.

Alariel: This gives a good overview of the Essene way of healing, and you will notice that the traditional term, 'laying on of hands' does not even occur here in the list of Essene skills. Of course, channeling energy through the hands occurred frequently in Essene healing processes, but this was considered such a basic aspect of healing that the Essenes took it for granted to the point that it need not be mentioned.

However, we should not give the impression that healing had become such a common routine for the Essenes that they 'went through the motions' in a dull, mechanical fashion. Before beginning the healing, the healer would tune in (as best he or she could) to the soul of the patient to ask if healing was appropriate at that time. This attunement was not merely a polite formality—it had a profound purpose, and when we consider how Jeshua carried out this initial stage, we will understand it better. Jeshua raised the healing techniques of the Essenes to a higher level, and that is demonstrated even at this initial stage in the process.

Jeshua's ability to tune into the soul of the patient was incomparably better than any other Essene. He could hold an extended unspoken dialogue with the soul at a multidimensional level so that it took no linear time, and this gave him a clear picture of how to proceed. What Jeshua needed to know was how extensive—in terms of the vehicles of consciousness involved—and how long-lived—in terms of the lives in which this problem had occurred—that health condition really was. The key to a healing process is to understand where the problem comes from, how far it has spread, and how long it has been in the patient's system.

A problem resulting from disharmony generated in this life is one thing; a problem resulting from a disharmonic pattern that has recurred in several past lives and has worked its way down from the mental or emotional level into the physical body is quite another thing. When spiritual lessons are stubbornly refused in lifetime after lifetime, the illness that is generated at the physical level becomes highly resistant to resolution into a state of final harmony until the whole being—personality as well as soul—has fully mastered that lesson and is ready to move on.

Jeshua was sensitive to the position of both the personality and the soul concerning the illness, and this ability gave him a complete understanding of how close the personality-plus-soul unit was to reaching a breakthrough which might result in the underlying spiritual lesson being learned. If that opportunity for a breakthrough was close, he would not attempt to heal the person at all because to do so might run counter to the wishes of the soul by perpetuating the underlying problem. In these circumstances, the kindest thing that could be done was *to do nothing* and let the breakthrough take place.

However, assuming that the soul consented to healing because no imminent spiritual breakthrough was involved, Jeshua could then proceed by using any of the techniques we have been considering and a few others beyond this, including total immersion in water. And yes, there was often the channeling of energies through the hands and sometimes the use of sound in the form of chants or prayers. Yet beyond all of these techniques, there was an overarching and unifying foundation for the healing, something that once again Daniel has summed up very well.

Daniel: The healer holds the vision of the person before him as a perfect being, completely aligned with the Divine pattern. Whatever illness may be present, this pattern always remains perfect, and the healer affirms that perfection. Then the healer invokes the power of the Spirit to flow down into the pattern and to link it with the projection which is the physical body.

Advanced healers are able to do this effectively because they have cleared away all the obstacles within themselves and have become perfect channels for this power. When the Spirit moves to manifest perfection, all else in the universe steps aside.

Alariel: *Now* do you see how complete the process of healing was when undertaken by a Master-Soul like Jeshua? Many Essenes were able to master some aspects of this process, but Jeshua alone had the knowledge and the skill necessary to bring all this together at the highest level of accomplishment. He certainly worked within the established Essene healing tradition, but he also moved it on, perfected it, and demonstrated its full and realized potential.

Comment by Stuart: The use of a musical analogy here is interesting. Daniel talks about "re-attunement to the essential note of the individual," and Alariel uses the phrase "resolution into a state of final harmony." Seeing a human being as a holistic system with harmonic possibilities is certainly a fascinating idea, and the expression of well-being might then be perceived as a state of musical harmony within the system as a whole.

7. Joseph as the Connecting Thread

One thread runs through the whole Essene story, and that is the presence of Joseph of Arimathea. It is Joseph who oversees the construction of the tunnel, Joseph who masterminds the healing in the tomb, and Joseph who gets Jeshua safely out of Israel. Jeshua may have been the central character in the drama, but none of this would have happened without Joseph working away in the background, smoothing over the differences, and encouraging the Essenes to work together for the greater good. Our Essene narrative starts with Joseph (and his friend Daniel), and so it seems appropriate to reconnect here with Joseph in this, the third and last of our Essene books.

Although Joseph's efficiency was legendary—and essential to the whole drama—one aspect of it still remained a mystery to us. How did he control his large shipping fleet without the help of modern communications? When we asked Alariel about that, this was his response.

Alariel: The commercial shipping fleet controlled by Joseph varied in size from 120 to about 150 ships. As a number of these would always be in a process of repair and refitting, this meant that his total fleet was never fully available at any one time. Joseph was careful to build surplus capacity into his fleet for two reasons. Firstly, it enabled him to respond instantly to urgent orders from the Roman military, and secondly, it gave him spare ships to carry passengers amongst the Essenes and the disciples when they needed transport. By building this surplus cushion of capacity into his shipping system, Joseph was able to run his fleet on a basis that was both efficient and also relatively low-key and relaxed.

Whilst other merchants shipping other goods might put stress on their employees through striving for the larger short-term profits that come with running a lean system, Joseph took the long view. His policy of allowing ample margins of capacity gave his fleet a sense of smooth and routine operation that was the envy of all those who knew about shipping in that era. And this wise and benign policy, extended over time, enabled him to recruit the best people who were more loyal to him than to any other ship owners. He simply knew how to treat his people fairly, and this fair-dealing resulted in a remarkably high level of loyalty amongst his staff.

But to understand how this commercial shipping empire was controlled, you would need to see the system at work, so let me take you now on a visual tour of Joseph's large house in

Jerusalem. This was laid out upon three floors. The ground floor contained reception areas, the main family rooms, and utility areas like the kitchen. On the middle floor the family had their bedrooms, and there were guest rooms for the frequent visitors. But the real center of Joseph's operations and the place where he spent most of his time was the top floor.

At one end of the building, there was an outside staircase allowing his staff to access the top floor without going through the family rooms on the lower floors. From this staircase you came first to several small storerooms and then on the right hand side to Joseph's large and well-furnished office, which overlooked the gardens at the back of the house. Beyond this office, a glazed door gave into the main room on this floor, a long room with a large window covering most of the end wall with stained glass panels in Joseph's favorite colors of yellow and brown.

As you enter this room two things strike you at once. Firstly, all along the left hand wall, there are wooden pigeon-holes and in front of these are desks for the scribes and at the far end a larger one for the office manager.

When a travelling scroll is brought in from an incoming ship, a scribe makes a brief digest of its contents in a big scroll called 'The Report for the Day,' which is consulted by Joseph whenever he enters the room. The traveling scrolls are small, and Joseph encouraged all his staff to write briefly and concisely. Each traveling scroll came with its own thin copper tube, and after it had been processed by the scribe, it was filed in the appropriate pigeon-hole, this being labeled with the number of the ship. Joseph knew that a combination of a single letter and a two-digit number would be easier for his staff to remember, and so that was the system that was used to identify ships.

But it was the second feature of this large room which made the greatest impression on any visitor. The whole of the right-hand wall from above shoulder height down to about knee level was covered in a series of wooden panels, seamlessly joined together and painted in blue to represent the Mediterranean (which they called 'the Central Sea') and in green to represent the land around it. However, as Joseph was a practical man, he made no attempt at geographical accuracy when designing this large wooden Display. He was only interested in the ports, so the whole area of Gaul (the present-day France) was reduced to a thin strip of land. Through this means he could show Britain up as far as just north of Avalon and with all his Cornish tin mines marked, and Gaul, and all the ports around the Mediterranean.

Each port was marked with a plaque showing its name in Hebrew and in Roman script, for it was this Display that Joseph used to impress visiting Roman officials. Into the plaque for each port were placed small wooden labels, these showing which ships were calculated to have reached that destination. And at the far end of the Display, there was a Key listing the letter-and-number code alongside the name of the ship and the name of its captain. There were also small round holes at intervals along the main sea-routes, and in these, special markers were placed to show the estimated location of ships.

Of course, ships were sometimes lost at sea, even in the Mediterranean, which was noted for storms that blew up quickly. That was another good reason for keeping ships always at the ready: when news of a shipwreck came, a rescue vessel could be dispatched at once to try to locate survivors. Joseph had the reputation of a man who always looked after his own people.

To the Pharisees in the Sanhedrin, it must have seemed that Jerusalem was the undoubted center of Joseph's world, but, in truth, it was Cyprus that was the hub of his operations. And when Joseph had to leave in haste, he went first to his great friend amongst the Roman administrators to arrange for an escort of a Centurion and six Roman soldiers. Then Joseph set off hurriedly within the hour, and when he went, he went alone. But when Joseph's family and his staff left early the following morning, they left with the Roman escort, and in their baggage carts they carried all of Joseph's files—files which would have greatly interested those conducting the

Sanhedrin investigation into Joseph and all his links with the group around Jeshua, links which were by then arousing ever greater suspicion.

It was within the context of these investigations that a representative of the Sanhedrin called in the early afternoon, but to his great surprise, he found Joseph's house deserted and littered with all the signs of a hasty departure.

The only person there was Joseph's friend Nicodemus, and he showed the Pharisee round the empty house and the *very* empty office with great courtesy—but with a knowing smile upon his face!

8. A Turning Point

The crucifixion was a turning point in several ways. It marked the end of the Essene Brotherhood's big project of supporting Jeshua, their Teacher of Righteousness, as he completed the energy cycle and anchored the energy of Love into the matrix of the Earth. This made the Christ energy—the energy of Unconditional Love—accessible to all those who are open to bringing change and transformation into their lives. This energy had always been available to advanced initiates in the Mystery Schools since the time of Atlantis when Jeshua in one of his female incarnations focused this energy for the first time, drawing it from its Cosmic source into the spiritual sphere of the Earth. (An account of this Atlantean process is given in our book *Atlantis and the New Consciousness*.)

Alariel has told us that the crucifixion marked the end of a vast cycle of spiritual development. Here he is describing this in chapter 12 of *Power of the Magdalene*.

Alariel: The point at which Jeshua was born was the very nadir of spirituality on this planet, the lowest point of the devolutionary arc. Because Jeshua and Mary Magdalene moved human consciousness forward into an upward spiral, this opened up many new opportunities for human beings to rise in vibration and access higher levels of consciousness, subtler frequencies of Light and being, that would not have been possible within the previous downward spiral.

By turning the devolutionary spiral into an upward evolutionary one, Jeshua and Mary saved humanity from a long period of experience at a much lower level . . . Jeshua and Mary Magdalene saved humanity from the possibility of future sins, not the burden of past Karma. They saved you from all the sins that would have been committed if the darkness had continued to spread and the downward arc of devolution had not been turned into the upward arc of spiritual evolution. Jeshua and Mary Magdalene are the combined saviors of humanity and should be honored as such.

Comment by Stuart: In a sense the crucifixion also signaled the end of the whole development of Essene communities, and it was the beginning of the end of the whole Essene way of life. Both the tradition—and many of the personnel—would go on into the Gnostic movement, but when the elders met for the last time in a cave after the crucifixion, they knew in their hearts that the great days of the Essene tradition were over.

That meeting (described in chapter 43 of *The Essenes: Children of the Light*) was addressed by the senior member of the Melchizedek Order upon this planet, and after thanking all present for the efforts that had been made, he went on to say that this meeting "Marked the end of the Essene Order's outer and visible role in the world . . . And the achievements . . . were considerable. The communities had been well-founded and well-run and had given several generations of Essenes an experience of Star Wisdom. Many souls had been helped upon the path to the Light, and much knowledge had been gathered and circulated. The Teacher of Righteousness had been helped by an excellent supporting organization, making his task much easier. That task had now been completed . . . the cosmic energies had been gathered and brought into synthesis, ending one great cycle of human development, and the new love-energy had been firmly established upon the Earth."

Comment by Stuart: But there were other shifts occurring at this time at a more personal level. Those close to Jeshua—and especially those who stood at the foot of the cross—sustained a huge emotional trauma which took some of them centuries, and many more lives on Earth, to resolve. Indeed, it is true to say that those who bore the brunt of the emotional shock of the crucifixion are in some cases still working on this process of healing and resolution.

This was underlined in the N.L.P. process called "Changing Negative Beliefs" facilitated by the holistic therapist Emma (whose account of her life as Laura Clare is given in *Power of the Magdalene*.) "Changing Negative Beliefs" is a process by which the participant focuses on a "Negative Belief" . . . identifies the emotions attached to the belief . . . recognizes when he/she first felt these emotions . . . realizes the "Good Intentions" of all those concerned . . . sees the "Good Outcome" . . . and forms a "New Belief."

Late in August 2010, Emma facilitated an N.L.P. session with my friend Janie, and because Janie is able to access the Akashic Records, she was able to lift the emotional energy from her present life and connect this with her life 2,000 years ago in Israel. (The Akashic Records are the angelic system of recording all actions and thoughts. This system is used by the angelic host to administer the process of Karma.) Here is Janie's powerful and very moving account.

Janie: We are huddled here at the foot of cross. We have become like 'clothed boulders.' We are curled up in pain, unable to unfurl, kneel, or stand because of the extreme agony.

There is so much confusion. There are so many feelings and emotions: feelings of abandonment and desertion, feelings of shame and guilt, feelings of failure and injustice.

Emma: *We can't do anything to stop this. He is going to die. We should have protected him. Why couldn't we protect him?*

Janie: The Savior's 'Good Intention' was to anchor Light into the planet. (The extent of our grief had not been foreseen, and the effect of our grief upon him made his task so much more difficult.)

The Essenes' 'Good Intention' was to love and protect their Savior. (They couldn't save their Savior.)

The 'Good Intention' of the crucifiers was to restore their authority. They had been so afraid of this intangible energy coming from Jesus. They knew only swords and armor as power.

There were several 'Good Outcomes.' There was the empowering of the female (which became Mary Magdalene's task.) If Jesus had not gone, the female energy could not have surfaced. If he had not gone, the female energy could not have been empowered. If he had still been 'there,' the male and female Essene energy would have stayed in Israel, and the Light could not have gone out all over the world. It had to go to Cyprus, to India, to Avalon, to Languedoc.

If we had known that he had survived and gone to India, we would have followed him and held him in the density of our grief. How could the grief, the anger, and the hurt be taken to India? How could he have worked there in purity if we had gone with him? He had to let go of the grief because he had to work in purity—we would not have been able to do that.

The Essene women had compassion and support in their grief, but it was the compassion and support from the men that was of great significance. The men alone in the consciousness of that time could not experience all the emotions of compassion, love, and loss. But in their role as 'protectors of the women,' they could feel the emotions coming from the grieving community of women and express them as their own.

As to the bigger picture (if we had but seen it), it was all about 'letting go' and 'moving on.'

Now as we approach the end of this planetary cycle, the emotions are intensifying in our everyday lives as we endeavor to move rapidly through our Karma. It is time to release patterns of abandonment, desertion, shame, guilt, failure and injustice. It is time to trust that the angels will always help, if we simply ask.

So the 'New Belief' is that it is all part of the Divine Plan and that the Divine Plan does exist. We need Faith and Trust and Expansion. After that life in Israel we expanded out over the world, taking the Light of Christ Consciousness with us. By knowing Jesus and his energy, we were able to carry that with us.

It's also about knowing and trusting in the Abundance. The Abundance of Joseph of Arimathea was to safeguard the passage of Jesus and many other Essenes.

To break up the 'closed' Essene communities was scary, but we had to be scattered to take the energy that we each held. If you experience an energy that is that light and that pure, you hold and communicate some of that energy just by being in its memory.

Comment by Stuart: I am so grateful both to Janie and to Emma, who as a holistic therapist was able to facilitate this remarkable session. It illuminates so much of what was going on emotionally at that time in Israel, and it explains why this was such a turning point.

Judaism at that time in history had intensified the patriarchal energy to such a degree that it had reached the absolute limit of its capacity, and the pendulum *had* to swing back towards the Sacred Feminine in general and the empowerment of individual women in particular. Emotionally, this was the big turning point—it showed that the first cracks were starting to appear in the monolithic and rigid ancient Jewish patriarchy. And it also revealed the first tentative steps being taken towards a new balance in the relationship between men and women—a balance which, 2,000 years later, we are still developing and perfecting.

9. The Identity of Mary Magdalene

When we read *Anna, The Voice of the Magdalenes* by Claire Heartsong and Catherine Ann Clemett, a number of questions came up for us, particularly about the concept that Mary Magdalene was a composite of three individuals in the Order of the Magdalene: Myriam of Tyana, Mary of Bethany and Mariam of Mount Carmel. This was Alariel's response to our enquiries.

Alariel: There certainly was an Order of the Magdalene of which Myriam of Tyana, Mary of Bethany, and Mariam Joanna of Mount Carmel were the Founders and core members. However, there was only one wife and spiritual partner of Jeshua, and that was Myriam of Tyana. Such was the dedication and the complete spiritual integration of these original three core members of this Order that it sometimes happens that subsequent incarnations of these souls—or aspects of these souls— remember 'being Mary Magdalene,' and this has caused some degree of confusion.

So Mary Magdalene was Myriam of Tyana, and it is Myriam that we have concentrated on in the information provided for *Power of the Magdalene* and this present book. We hope this explanation will clarify the position on this key area of identity.

Comment by Stuart: Here Joanna adds some further words that I think will bring clarity to this area.

Joanna: It's important not to get caught up too much in 'who-was-who.' It's time we all pulled together and stopped arguing about these details. In any case, it is more complex now as many people are soul aspects rather than full incarnations—a subject we touched on in Chapter 4 of *Power of the Magdalene.* And there are other possibilities:

1. Being over-lighted by the original being;
2. Tuning in to the Akashic Records;
3. Tuning in to the Collective Unconscious;
4. Remembering a life when one was close to the key character.

The session with Alariel continues.

Alariel: When you asked about the identity of Mary Magdalene towards the end of last year, we could give only a little information on this subject because we respect the team who have been working on *Anna, The Voice of the Magdalenes* and did not wish to 'steal their thunder' by giving out information on the Order of the Magdalene prematurely. Now that this significant book is safely published, we can give a good deal more information on Mary Magdalene's background.

Mary (or Myriam to give the original form of her name) was born into a Jewish family of the tribe of Benjamin. This branch of the tribe had traveled from Israel and eventually settled in Tyana, an ancient Hittite city, which is mentioned in several Assyrian texts. Tyana is located in what is now the south-central region of Turkey between the Black Sea and the Mediterranean.

Mary's grandfather was Balthazar, one of the Three Wise Men, and he came from Persia. Her father, a wealthy merchant called James, had met Joseph of Arimathea on his travels and became his friend, and when James died while Mary was still a child, Joseph adopted her and brought her to Israel. Mary was eight years old when her father died, and she came to live in Joseph of Arimathea's large and comfortable house in Jerusalem. A frequent visitor to that house was Joseph's nephew Jeshua, then eleven years old. Mary and Jeshua developed an intense friendship and became aware of a powerful spiritual bond that extended over many lifetimes. They had one magical year together before Jeshua went off at the age of twelve on his longer journeys, culminating in his trip to India, and Mary went to train at the Isis Temple in Alexandria.

When they met again on his return from India, Jeshua had become a fully-fledged Initiate of the Ageless Wisdom, so that he had reached the level of High Priest, and Mary had risen to become a High Priestess in the Isis tradition.

These two advanced and enlightened Beings came together at that time as spiritual equals in a partnership of profound significance for the world, and being each of High Priest/Priestess level, their energies had become remarkably focused and powerful. When you reach that level, your consciousness automatically generates a twelve-pointed transformational vortex around you, a vortex of change so powerful that it will cause ripples of change in the consciousness of all those who are anywhere near you.

When two vortexes of transformation are in the same proximity, the interconnection of energies boosts the combined power so that they form an energetic focus so powerful that—to the vision of angels, at least—they appear as a great beacon of Light that is visible throughout the entire galaxy. Now can you begin to see why Mary and Jeshua, working closely together at the time of the Ministry, had such a powerful effect on those they encountered! Two people of High Priest/Priestess level working together in perfect harmony are very rare upon the Earth. It happened with Francis of Assisi and St Clare, but it is a rare event of major significance for the planet.

When Jeshua was speaking to a large crowd of people and Mary Magdalene was present, energetically their relationship was like Shiva and his Shakti, Parvati. The Hindus wisely perceived that the Divine Masculine provides structure and focus while the Divine Feminine provides the energy to boost and sustain the process. When Jeshua was speaking to a crowd, even though Mary said nothing, she was a vital part in this process since her transformational vortex—linked with Jeshua's—provided a complete communication system. That communication carried in words, in energy, and in *mudras* (special hand gestures) the principle of which Jeshua had learned in India and developed in his unique fashion—provided a multi-level expression. Even if you were deaf, the energy and the *mudras* would give you the whole message. And even if you were *deaf and blind* the energy of these two combined transformational vortexes could reach you and change your life forever.

Comment by Stuart: The reference to special hand gestures was interesting, but at first I only saw this as a way of communicating the spoken ideas within a different format. However, when I saw our friend Josee Honeyball facilitate a Matrix Energetics session for Joanna, it occurred to me that Jeshua might have been using his hands to work multi-dimensionally with his audience. (Matrix Energetics is a form of energy medicine that applies the principles of quantum physics. It was developed by Dr. Richard Bartlett. See www.matrixenergetics.com) When I asked Alariel to comment on this possibility, he gave this response.

Alariel: When Jeshua was speaking to an audience, his hand gestures did support the spoken message, but he was also working energetically on higher levels. Many of those who watched him speak noticed that his eyes seemed to focus just above the heads of his audience, and if I tell you what he was seeing, the reason for this will become clear.

As he looked out over the assembled crowd, Jeshua could see the architecture of consciousness rise up in a semi-transparent form above the head of each individual. These were people raised within a single, intense, and monolithic culture, and that culture had shaped and molded each consciousness upon similar lines. So within each form that the consciousness projected, there were similar colors and almost identical patterns of movement. Within the architecture of each consciousness-form could be seen similar areas of blocking and resistance to change and similar patterns of restriction and rigidity.

By using hand gestures backed up by the power of the transformational vortex created by his own consciousness, Jeshua was able to work simultaneously on several levels to release the blocks in the consciousness of all those who were present. Because the crowds were often tightly packed around him, leading to an overlapping at the auric level, this meant that the wave of transformation could spread through the crowd with the rapidity of a forest fire. And as blocks were released and a more natural openness and flow were restored to consciousness, Jeshua could see the result in shifts in color frequency and changes in form and pattern.

Perhaps the high level of Jeshua's multi-dimensional skills is now becoming clear: you simply cannot compare this deeply transformational experience with hearing a learned rabbi expounding upon the details of the Jewish Law!

Comment by Stuart: Here is another example of the depth of Alariel's understanding moving the whole subject into multi-dimensional areas which we would never have been able to access without his help. And, indeed, the whole of this section was intriguing, including the reference to Balthazar, so we asked Alariel to expand on this.

Alariel: Balthazar was a member of the Brotherhood of Light and a long term friend and colleague over many lives of the soul who became Joseph of Arimathea. This established a link between Joseph and Mary Magdalene *even before she was born*. This is why the family of Myriam allowed Joseph to adopt her—they recognized that in doing so, they were

73

fulfilling the wishes of her grandfather, who they greatly respected, and they saw that this was part of a much bigger sequence of events that were unfolding for the greater good.

Comment by Stuart: The vortex of energies reference is also fascinating. This kind of energetic effect on a much more modest level can be seen when any two spiritual partners work together in harmony for the greater good.

I am greatly indebted to Catherine Mary La Toure at whose house I channeled Alariel in December 2009. At that point we had a brief glimpse of some of this information, but it expanded to its present form in October 2010 following the publication of Claire Heartsong's second book earlier that year.

When we started to absorb all this new information from Alariel, another question came into focus for us: if the consciousness of a High Priest automatically creates this kind of transformational vortex, why didn't this happen in the case of the High Priest in the Temple in Jerusalem? This was Alariel's reply to that question.

Alariel: The consciousness only creates this vortex providing the High Priest or Priestess *continues serving the Light.* In the case of Caiaphas, the High Priest at that time, he turned from a focus on the Light towards a focus on worldly power. Had he *continued* to focus on the Light, the whole of your planet's history would have been profoundly changed. Then he would have become Jeshua's most prominent disciple, and there would have been no crucifixion, no persecution of the Gnostics, no Crusade against the Cathars—but perhaps also no Christianity as you know it. If instead of *any* kind of Christianity, there was simply a reformed branch of Judaism, would you be happy with that outcome? Perhaps you might not be comfortable with this parallel history either! Timelines as we explained in your third book are extremely complex, and small changes in the present may have profound consequences in future-time.

Comment by Stuart: In saying "your third book," Alariel is indicating *Beyond Limitations: The Power of Conscious Co-Creation.* This contains a chapter, "Timelines and Lifelines," which expands upon this theme.

One further piece of information about Mary's parents came to us in February 2011 during a session when our friend Sue Fraser and I both channeled. At that time it became clear that Mary's stepmother remained in Tyana to look after Mary's younger brother, secure in the knowledge that a supportive network would be put in place around Mary by the ever-thorough Joseph.

10. The Gnostic World

The world into which the Gnostics came was essentially a world in ferment. Whereas the Essenes had a period of relative calm and stability from 170 BCE to the birth of Jeshua to establish their main communities in Damascus, Alexandria and Qumran, Israel in the first century was a land in turmoil. The Zealots were fomenting widespread unrest, which flared up into a full-scale rebellion against Roman rule in 66 CE. The next few years were a time of chaos, and it is against this background of political unrest and spiritual ferment that the Gnostic movement emerged. When asked about the Gnostics, this was Alariel's reply.

Alariel: This was a very broad-based movement with major differences between the Christian and Jewish Gnostics and a variety of views even within these two branches. Some of the elements of Gnostic thought predated the rise of Christianity, and that makes it difficult to put this whole subject into any kind of rigid category.

Then there is the question of Gnostic theology, which has always been controversial. It is not true that all

Gnostics believed in a dual creation although some Gnostics certainly did. And the idea of heaven created by God and the material world created by a lesser divine being—the 'Demiurge'—would now seem very strange, indeed, to most people in the West. To the Gnostics, theology was just a series of mind-games that their most brilliant thinkers liked to indulge in.

Theology was a diversion to the Gnostics, not the heart of things as it was for the mainstream Christian followers of Peter and Paul. The Gnostics knew that it was process—the following of the Way— that really mattered. If process could take you into enlightenment and ascension, what value would you put on theology in comparison to that?

In any case, there was no general agreement on theology amongst Gnostic thinkers. Yes, some of them supported the dualistic creation featuring the Demiurge, but progressive Gnostics like Mary Magdalene certainly did not, and there is no trace of dualism in her statements— quite the reverse. In fact, there is a continual returning to the theme of Oneness.

Although there were Gnostics scattered over much of the Middle East, there was a big concentration of Gnostic groups in Egypt, significantly the country where many Gnostic texts have been discovered. And within Egypt, the groups in Alexandria were particularly advanced and influential.

The Jewish Gnostics in Alexandria could trace their roots back to the large Essene community in that area, disbanded by the latter part of the first century but still very much an aspect of the oral tradition there. It is important to remember that for generations the Essenes both in Egypt and in Israel had sent their brightest daughters for training to the Isis Temple in Alexandria.

Comment by Stuart: When we produced our second book, *Power of the Magdalene,* we discovered that Mary Magdalene had not only been trained in that temple but continued to be a regular visitor there as the experience of Akhira in Chapter 7 showed. Mary became a mentor for a whole generation of girls who were being trained in the Isis tradition, and they very much looked forward to her visits. Over a period of time she became almost like an elder sister to them—someone who had passed through the same training and could be a source of encouragement and wise guidance.

The session with Alariel continues.

Alariel: The principal difference between the mainstream Christian Church and the Gnostics was the contrast between doctrine and process. For Christians in the tradition of Peter and Paul, doctrine was at the heart of their faith, but for the Gnostics, the key to treading the spiritual path was a process which they called 'The Way.' This they considered to be the very heart of the teaching that Jeshua had given. This was knowledge that could liberate you, the Truth that could set you free.

John was the only disciple who managed to maintain links with both the Gnostic movement and the emergent mainstream Christian Church. Because his support for Peter was consistent and unwavering, he was considered to be one of the three great 'pillars' of the early Church, alongside Peter and James the Just. In this work John was fulfilling a pledge given to Jeshua that he would be a peacemaker and try to form a bridge between the two developing strands: the Outer Church led by Peter and the Inner Mystery School led by Mary Magdalene.

Comment by Stuart: This division into Church and Mystery School is described in Chapter 11 of our book *Power of the Magdalene*.

The session with Alariel continues.

Alariel: Although John was more inclined in his heart to follow the inner-focused path of the Gnostics, he was critical of some of their theoretical foundations. In particular, he recognized that the idea of a dualistic creation was wrong—dangerously wrong. He spoke out against it wherever he encountered it in Gnostic groups as he traveled and wrote against it when he sent letters to outlying groups. John told the Gnostics that by labeling the Earth and the physical body as a degenerate and lesser creation, they were storing up trouble for themselves. He said that to take that line might encourage the belief that the physical body was unspiritual at best and evil at worst and that this way of thinking could lead to the punishment and mortification of the flesh.

In John's view, all of Creation down to and including the physical body was the handiwork of the true God, and he emphasized that through balanced expression at the physical level, we learn and grow spiritually. Thus physical experience forms part of our spiritual journey, the journey of the soul, and it should not be despised and denigrated. To do that would be to despise and denigrate part of God's Creation, which for a spiritual person would surely be illogical.

Of all Jeshua's disciples, John and Mary Magdalene were the most advanced. These were the two 'beloved disciples' whose understanding went far beyond that of the most conventional followers like Peter and Andrew. Yet Jeshua advised John and Mary to value Peter, for he could relate to the common man and speak in terms that the average person could understand. This is why Jeshua had chosen Peter to lead the outer Church, for he was a fiery and charismatic speaker with this vital common touch that enabled him to bridge the gap between spiritual philosophy (which interested only the intellectual few) and the practical spreading of the good news (which was a project in which many could take part and benefit from.)

Comment by Stuart: It's easy to be critical of Peter and his brother Andrew as the slow learners in the group of disciples, but actually Peter was very effective at doing what he alone could do.   No, he wasn't a shining intellect like John and Mary Magdalene, but he was a brilliant mass-communicator who could talk in terms that the great majority of the people could understand. Without Peter there might have been no Church and no Christianity at all.   The movement might have fragmented into twenty or thirty competing Gnostic, Roman-Hellenic and Jewish-Christian groups.   And all of these small splinter groups might have been overwhelmed by the powerful religious opposition that existed at that time.

We now live in a world where there are just a few major religious groups, but the world of Jeshua's time was very different.   Then there were *hundreds* of religions, some operating on a one-tribe basis with a god or goddess unique to and protective of that tribe.   But there were also powerful pagan religions, some inspiring fanatical loyalty amongst their adherents.

Without Peter's inspired leadership, the battle could easily have been lost, and Christianity could have disappeared in the very first century, overwhelmed by its pagan opposition.   If that had happened, we would now know no more about Christianity than we know about all the hundreds of forgotten faiths—a few artifacts, some written fragments but nothing substantial.   So think about this when you think of Peter: without him the world might have been quite a different place.

The session with Alariel continues.

Alariel: On many occasions Jeshua talked with John and Mary Magdalene alone, and they knew his innermost thoughts and the full extent of his philosophy. And because of this special closeness to Jeshua, John and Mary Magdalene became linked together as Brother and Sister in the Light. That is why it so hurt John when he heard the conventional disciples, especially Andrew and his brother Peter, criticize Mary and try to diminish her standing amongst the disciples.

Comment by Stuart: In the light of what Alariel says here, it is interesting to note that John and Mary Magdalene are identified as the most advanced disciples in the Gnostic text *Pistis Sophia*. When the rest of the disciples collapse exhausted by the strenuous process of dialogue on the most difficult and complex subjects, John and Mary Magdalene remain eager to question Jeshua and arrive at the truth. Jeshua says that Mary Magdalene and John "Will tower over all my disciples." (See the Hurtak translation, page 513.)

The session with Alariel continues.

Alariel: Throughout his life John was always Mary's friend and defender, even more understandable when one considers that they shared an Essene upbringing and were both members of the Core Group, a secret group that lay at the very heart of the Essene Brotherhood.

Comment by Stuart: The Core Group was a highly secret inner circle of Essenes who were dedicated to supporting the work of Jeshua and to ensuring—as much as they could—his safety. The Core Group is described in Chapter 16 of our book *The Essenes: Children of the Light.*

The session with Alariel continues.

Alariel: Coming from this shared Essene background and growing in spiritual stature together under Jeshua's guidance, John and Mary developed a strong bond based on friendship and respect. Andrew and Peter resented their closeness to Jeshua and would have liked to criticize and diminish both of them, but such was John's standing in the respect of all the other disciples that this was out of the question. And that is why they often criticized Mary, for she seemed the easier target.

In a sense their mistrust of John and Mary was deeply rooted in a two-fold emotion: they were baffled by their subtle understanding of spiritual ideas too lofty and philosophical for more basic minds to grasp, and they resented being excluded from this inner circle of Jeshua's most favored and beloved disciples. A powerful envy gnawed away at Andrew and Peter and fueled their resentment of John and Mary.

Comment by Stuart: The picture of Mary Magdalene that emerges from the Gnostic texts is a powerful one. In *The Dialogue of the Savior,* Mary Magdalene makes a very confident statement (in 139:11-13), and the author of this text adds. "She said this as a woman who understands the All." This turns out to be a key description of Mary, and one that will gain much greater significance as this account unfolds. (In some translations, the words "the All" are replaced by "completely." A study of the Gnostic text *Pistis Sophia* will show that "the All" is clearly the better translation.)

11. Church and Mystery School

When we were producing our second book, *Power of the Magdalene,* we encountered a really significant piece of information—Jeshua had intended his disciples to set up a two-fold structure that was a lot more subtle and effective than the Church that actually emerged. Here (from chapter 11 in that book) is our angelic source Alariel explaining this.

Alariel: Peter could not accept the basic structure through which the Way would be spread— that after Jeshua left them, the teachings would be given out in two ways. The outer teachings would be spread by most of the male disciples, led by Peter, who was to be *the rock,* the foundation, of this new movement. Whilst the inner teachings (the Inner Mysteries of the Way) would be taught by John, James, Thomas and Philip with this group led by Mary Magdalene. Mary . . . saw the two teaching arms as mutually supportive because the outer group would be open and public and would deflect attention away from the inner, which, in any case, needed a quieter environment to do the subtle work along esoteric and Gnostic lines . . .

After the crucifixion when James and Mary tried to explain this two-part plan to Peter, he brushed it off at once as impractical. He saw the followers of Jeshua as an embattled army and regarded any kind of division as a splitting and weakening of their forces. Besides, Peter could not tolerate the idea of a rival leader, and a rival leader who happened to be a woman was quite unthinkable for him.

Comment by Stuart: And here is Alariel bringing this forward and moving it on into the Gnostic era.

Alariel: Despite Peter's opposition, the inner Mystery School did go ahead with Mary Magdalene as its leader. Mary set up this organization to function on three levels:

1. Weekly Groups meeting wherever they arose;

2. Quarterly Meetings in a central location within each country, so that the emergent Gnostic groups could share ideas and learn from each other;

3. Annual Gatherings held on the estate of Joseph of Arimathea on the island of Cyprus. Joseph provided both transport for Gnostics attending these Gatherings through his vast network of ships carrying supplies of tin and a communication system centered on the Administrator's office on his estate. Through messages carried on the ships,

this office kept all the emergent Gnostic groups in contact with each other.

It was originally intended that the Gnostics involved in this Mystery School should meet every year, assembling on Midsummer's Day at Joseph of Arimathea's villa on Cyprus. However, these Gatherings could only occur when Mary Magdalene was available, and her busy schedule—including a journey to Britain, where she taught the Priestesses of Avalon—meant that in practice only eight of these Gatherings took place over a period of eleven years.

The knowledge given by Mary during these Gatherings was dramatically different from anything in the Gnostic Gospels: they represent the outer husk of the Gnostic movement, but what Mary Magdalene was giving in these Gatherings was the inner wisdom which remained secret. This wisdom was—from the very beginning—valued as being the most advanced and significant teachings that were available at that time.

12. The Existence of Secret Teachings

Alariel: Although the Gnostic Gatherings of the Mystery School took place on Joseph of Arimathea's estate, Joseph himself—due to his many other duties—was seldom present. And by the time these Gatherings were completed, everything had moved on. The disciples were scattered, and the Gnostics were beginning to establish a unique view of things that separated them from the conventional followers of Jeshua like Peter and Andrew.

Now that Jeshua was not physically present to inspire and guide, many in the Gnostic movement deferred to Mary Magdalene. She was the Keeper of the Flame of Truth, and it seemed quite natural for them to turn to her for guidance and counsel. Mary was widely respected as a source of Secret Wisdom, and for the progressive Gnostics she became a beacon of inspiration in what was becoming an increasingly difficult and dangerous world.

Throughout his Ministry, Jeshua had been aware of the weight of Jewish tradition upon his shoulders and the presence of the critical minds of the Pharisees just waiting for him to say something that they could use against him. Mary Magdalene in the Midsummer Gatherings on Cyprus had no such critical voices to contend with, so she could speak freely. And her thorough training as a High Priestess of Isis gave her a sense of detachment, enabling her to speak from a direct knowledge of inner wisdom.

After all her training and all the years with Jeshua, this was the time that Mary came into her own. She knew her own power and used it wisely. And her compassionate heart won her followers amongst all the groups who heard her speak. Here at last on the island of Cyprus she could speak all that was in her heart and mind, for here she was among colleagues and friends.

During each of the years when a Gathering was held, the participants, traveling on Joseph's ships, arrived from a number of locations, including Mary Magdalene from Languedoc, John from Israel and latterly from Ephesus, and Philip from Greece. Only the most open-minded and progressive Gnostics attended these Gatherings. They came from a range of backgrounds, Hellenic as well as Jewish-Essene, but they shared a passionate commitment to the Truth. The Gnostic groups in Greece included some of the most advanced and brilliant freethinkers of their age. The more conventional Gnostic groups, especially those close to the emergent mainstream Christian Church, chose not to attend these Gatherings. It was known from the beginning that Mary Magdalene would take a leading role in these Gatherings, and the more conventional Gnostics were uncomfortable with that format.

These Midsummer Gatherings were essentially the result of the collaboration between John and Mary Magdalene. John chaired the meetings, and Mary gave the central speech—I think these days you would call it a "Keynote Speech"—on the topic that had been agreed in advance as the central focus for that year's Gathering.

Joseph's estate on Cyprus was really the hub of his operations and a place of efficiency and order. Here the Gnostics could talk without being criticized and make their plans with no fear of persecution. The time spent in these Midsummer Gatherings was greatly valued by all who attended them, and Joseph of Arimathea (when he was present) and the Administrator who ran the estate (when Joseph was not) made sure that the guests lacked nothing.

The cool, well-furnished rooms in Joseph's large villa provided the ideal setting for these Gatherings. In the midsummer heat they were an oasis of calm in the midst of lives full of uncertainty and turmoil. Here the Gnostics could relax and consider their long-term plans, and these meetings became an opportunity to develop a theoretical and practical basis for the most advanced and progressive part of the Gnostic movement.

These Midsummer Gatherings all followed the same format. There would be a general sharing of information, a central speech by Mary Magdalene, and then wide-ranging discussion on the theme of that speech. And that discussion continued, not for days, but for several weeks. If it had taken you a week of uncomfortable travel to journey across the Middle East and arrive on this island, you would not rush away after a mere couple of days!

During each of the speeches, Mary explored one major theme, covering the ground thoroughly but concisely so that these speeches were known as "Summaries." These Summaries were never circulated to other groups, like documents such as *The Gospel of Mary,* and that is why no written form of them has survived into the present era.

Our angelic group, accessing the Akashic Records, has been working for some time on these Summaries, as we recognized that they spoke directly to a level of consciousness that was rare 2,000 years ago but is now becoming much more common. These Magdalene Summaries are, quite simply, texts whose time has come. That Mary Magdalene reached this advanced level 2,000 years ago gives some idea of how remarkable she was and how far ahead of the majority of Jeshua's disciples.

The Gnostic Gospels that have survived present very limited chances for Mary to expand on any theme. Within that context, she was never given the opportunity to make any kind of comprehensive statement of her philosophy on any subject. But here on the island of Cyprus, she has precisely that opportunity—and she seizes it with enthusiasm. If you want to know the depth and range of Mary's consciousness, you can find it here in these Magdalene Summaries, and nowhere else.

This is the real voice of Mary Magdalene— a voice that has not been heard for 2,000 years.

We must make one further point here. Knowledge of this kind was *never* taught at any point by the Christian Church. This is forbidden knowledge— forbidden by the Church because it might lead to gnosis and empowerment. The Church had no interest in producing enlightened and empowered beings who would challenge its authority. And when the last Gnostic died in the third century, most of this secret knowledge died with him. It continued to be taught in Mary's extended family group in Languedoc, but the teachers within that tradition became so few that they were unable over time to protect the purity of the Transmission.

This led to mistaken ideas, like the Dual Creation, creeping into the tradition by the time of the Cathars. The Cathars retained the *practice* of the Way, but by then their knowledge of Mary's philosophy had largely been lost. That is why the death of the last Gnostic marked the effective conclusion to this line of development as a Pure Transmission—a direct Transmission bringing Melchizedek wisdom to this planet. The Essenes were a Pure Transmission and so was Mary Magdalene's teaching in her Mystery School, but when the last Essene community was destroyed, and the last Gnostic died, that time of Pure Transmission came to an end.

That is why this process of recovery is so important: it restores the Pure Transmission of Mary Magdalene's teaching to the world. At the end of the planetary cycle, the veils of forgetting are dissolving, and knowledge that has been lost for many centuries is being restored. This teaching is one of the great jewels of human achievement, and with humanity moving through Transition, it is entirely right and just that access to it should be restored to you, as it may prove helpful at this time.

Comment by Stuart: This is one of the most important statements by Alariel because he is making it clear that the work of his angelic group in restoring this teaching to us is part of a greater process of support for humanity at the end of the planetary cycle. There is a profound sense of justice here: a vital part of our heritage that has long been lost to us is being restored at a critical time.

The session with Alariel continues.

Alariel: Here we must add a word on presentation. Instead of presenting these Magdalene Summaries in the simple but rather limited vocabulary which has become associated with that time, we have chosen to translate them into the more subtle and complex language that would now be used to discuss this kind of material. There are occasions when this more modern phrasing transforms the text, as one small example can demonstrate.

There is a passage in *The Gospel of Mary* where Jeshua is explaining that a vision is perceived through an aspect that links soul and Spirit, and in the text that aspect is called 'mind.' Now 'mind' is not the best term to use here because the mind only goes up as far as the soul and no higher, so it could never reach the level of Spirit. What can reach that level is consciousness, so 'consciousness' would be a more accurate term to use.

Comment by Stuart: There is a tabulation in Chapter 14 of our book *Beyond Limitations: The Power of Conscious Co-Creation* that makes Alariel's point clear. Significantly, the word 'consciousness' does not occur in the Authorized (King James)

Version of the Bible.

The session with Alariel continues.

Alariel: Information of the kind contained in these Magdalene Summaries has power in it because the Truth it contains carries an energy, and this energy can bring about changes in the consciousness. Humanity as a whole was not ready for this knowledge 2,000 years ago. It could be given to advanced seekers of the Truth like these Gnostics, but the great mass of people had not reached a level where this information could be absorbed and acted on. However, the planetary conditions are now very different. It is time for this Truth to go out into the world and for Mary Magdalene to be honored as the great soul that she is.

Comment by Stuart: It is quite difficult to assign accurate dates to these Midsummer Gatherings. The first problem is to determine a reliable date for the birth of Jeshua. Here there are several theories, but the most convincing date seems to be 5 BCE. During March and April in 5 BCE, the Chinese astronomers recorded the emergence of a nova—a new star—between the constellations of Capricorn and Aquila. This date also accords with the death of Herod a year later in 4 BCE. If Jeshua was born in 5 BCE, that would place his Ministry between 25 and 27 CE and the crucifixion at 27 CE.

We know there were eight of these Gatherings, but there were gaps in the program due to Mary's busy schedule, so the Gatherings were spread over eleven years. That would date these Gatherings to the years 28 to 38 CE.

The fresh information that has emerged through the channeling process gives us an opportunity to look at the teachings of Mary Magdalene in a new way. In the chapters that follow I give the complete text of the Magdalene Summaries as Alariel channeled them, together with any commentaries that he provided.

Part Two:

The Secret Teachings of Mary Magdalene

Everything is dual . . .
everything has its pair of opposites . . .
opposites are identical in nature
but different in degree.

Hermes-Thoth

13. The Inner Structure of Reality

Alariel: Concerning the Inner Structure of Reality, Mary Magdalene said this:

> This is what Jeshua taught me. He spoke of the very beginning of things, the inner structure of wisdom and the power of the Law of Three. He told me that before the world began, there were Three Great Trinities:
>> Father and Mother God create Light;
>> Light and Love create Spirit;
>> Spirit and Matter create Life.

> And Jeshua said that there are Trinities within Trinities, and this is a great mystery understood only by the wise. And he spoke of Love, which is the Christ, and he said the Christ also is a Trinity:

>> The Christ is the Energy of Love, and the nature of that Energy is redemption, healing, and Forgiveness.

>> The Christ is the Teacher, embodying this universal Energy.

The Christ is the awakened
Consciousness within the individual
that focuses through the heart.

So Jeshua told me that

the Christ is Energy;
the Christ is Teacher;
the Christ is Consciousness.

The Christ is the powerful Energy of
universal Love. This is Love for all beings,
and it is not hedged in and limited like
selfish love. This universal Love sweeps
away all boundaries and limitations, for
when the Christ Energy flows through your
being, all things are possible. And when
you understand the Christ Energy, you
begin to understand the nature of the All.

Father-Mother God and the Christ
are the essence of the One, the All.
Universal Oneness flows from this essence,
and so Creation is also One. When you
understand that the ultimate nature of
things is Oneness, you will see why all
forms must eventually return to that
nature. Oneness may flow into separation
at the physical level, but all things return
to their essence as Oneness when the cycle
of physical manifestation is complete.

The nature of Oneness is Light.
Creation flows from Light, descends into
the shadow-play of the material world for a
while and then ascends up again into
Light. That is why the soul must complete

its journey in Light. The soul came from Light, is Light, and to Light it will return.

Commentary by Alariel: *The concept of "Father-Mother God" would have horrified the Pharisees, but the Essenes were quite familiar with it—indeed, you could argue that the whole Essene philosophy was based upon the concept of the Heavenly Father and the Earthly Mother. One should always bear in mind that many of those who joined Gnostic groups at this period came from an Essene background or had sympathy with the Essene view of things. If they had grown up with these ideas in an Essene family, they would be quite comfortable with them.*

In this Magdalene Summary we get the full flavor of Mary's teaching. skill from the very beginning. Her style of presentation is direct, practical, and full of information, and she is not afraid to soar up into uplifting and inspirational statements.

To be both practical and inspirational is a rare and wonderful combination—and the secret of her power as a communicator.

Comment by Stuart: What is so remarkable about this Magdalene Summary is the way it introduces an entirely new theology. Mary puts forward a series of interlocking Trinities: a main structure of three Trinities and a subsidiary Trinity focusing on the Christ.

This may look radical—even revolutionary—to modern eyes, but it is important to remember that in the first two centuries of the Common Era there was no universally accepted perception of the Trinity. The elements of the modern Trinity were present, but their relationship was not fixed and determined during the first century.

Indeed, one can argue that it was only the Nicene Creed, agreed during the Council of Nicaea in 325 CE that established the Trinity in its modern form. Given the fluid nature of Christian theology in these early centuries, the existence of a radically different perception does not seem so strange or unreasonable.

When one considers this Magdalene Summary as a whole, it becomes clear that Mary Magdalene's object is not to establish faith or belief but to establish understanding. Yet the real surprise here is the directness and simplicity of her words. Much of Gnostic literature is obscure, archaic, and complex, littered with terms like "Aeons" and "Archons." In comparison, Mary's teaching—even at the most profound and abstract level—is direct and clear, and for that reason seems much more modern and accessible than most of the Gnostic literature.

14. The Sacred Universe

Alariel: Concerning the Sacred Universe, Mary Magdalene said this:

> We live in a sacred Universe where all things and all beings should be respected. If Father-Mother God created the Universe by *becoming* the Universe, one can understand why this should be so. Some of the most brilliant minds have doubted this, preferring to believe that this world, in general, and the physical level, in particular, is in some way lacking or inferior. I do not believe this as Father-Mother God has created all things, including the material world and the physical body; we should not despise any part of this creation.
>
> However, I can see the source of this confusion. As we pursue the spiritual path, the body does at times seem to be an obstacle and a hindrance upon this path, but to treat the body as the enemy is stupid and simplistic. When the body is trained and disciplined, it ceases to be an obstacle to spiritual progress and becomes instead like a friendly horse that will carry

you faithfully to your goal. If we are to exist effectively upon the physical level, we need the body as a vehicle to carry us along and enable us to achieve our aims; to despise and mortify this essential vehicle would surely be folly.

Working through the angelic host, Father-Mother God has created many marvels within the physical Universe. As we look at the landscape and the creatures that live in it, we are able to see only a small fraction of the wonders that exist right down to the minutest level. The angelic host has built a whole series of intricate mechanisms into even the smallest creature, and the more we look at the natural world, the more full of wonder and sacredness it becomes. The more you live in tune with the natural world, the more you begin to sense all the love that went into its creation. Look around you and you will see a world of beauty within a Universe of love.

As it is below in the world of physical matter, so it is above in the realm of Spirit. Remember that Jeshua said, "We are the Children of the Light and we came from the Light. And the balanced process of movement and repose is the sign of the Light within us." And he said also that the Creator planted within each Child of the Light a longing for the Light, so that even when lost in illusion, each would be able to find a path leading back to Father-Mother God. And Jeshua said, "The Way that I have taught you is that path leading to the Light."

> It is important to be clear about this: the Savior saves us from our ignorance of The Way, but we alone can save ourselves by following The Way and transforming our lives.

> If The Way remains a matter of knowledge and debate, it will have failed. It is a process and a path to tread. To succeed, The Way must become a living path of daily transformation. The fire of the Christ Consciousness must arise in our hearts, burning away all that is not Light. As we transform ourselves, we will help others to change, and an Awakening Humanity will help to transform the greater Stream of Life.
> To be transformed, Life must recognize the primacy of the Spirit, and matter must surrender to it. Then matter will transform into its root, which is Light, and return to the full embrace of the Spirit.

Commentary by Alariel: *Here Mary Magdalene reveals her complete dedication to the Spirit, the Light, the One. The passage concerning "the Savior" is particularly significant and may help to clarify an issue that has confused many people over the centuries.*

Mary quite firmly rejects the idea of a Dual Creation, which had so much currency within the Gnostic world of her time—an idea which saw God as creating the Heavens and a lesser being or

"Demiurge" as creating the Earth. By saying "God has created all things," she distances herself from this highly eccentric Gnostic viewpoint and affirms the integrity of the whole creation. In taking this stance, she was clearly reflecting Jeshua's own perception of things. Within the Gospel context, he never spoke of the Demiurge and gave no credence at all to the idea of a Dual Creation.

Looking back with hindsight, one can see how dangerous an idea this was. By regarding the world, in general, and the physical body, in particular, as an inferior and essentially sinful creation, the stage is set for a whole series of errors that would take the Western world away from the broad highway into the Light, which Jeshua was trying to establish.

Although the emergent mainstream Christian Church of Peter and Paul never subscribed to the Dual Creation idea, it did incorporate contempt for the physical level into both its theory and practice. Without this contempt, the monastic mortification of the flesh would not have arisen nor would the idea of a celibate priesthood have permeated through so many levels of the Church. It should be remembered that within the tradition which nurtured Jeshua—the Judaic tradition—rabbis were always married. Indeed, an unmarried rabbi would be considered unfit on the basis that he would be unable to counsel couples who were experiencing difficulties within their marriage.

There is another striking aspect of Mary Magdalene's statement here. She quotes from the Hermetic principle: "As above, so below." This is a clear reflection of her Essene background—the Essenes were perfectly familiar with the key Hermetic ideas, and these ideas had wide circulation in the Middle East at that time.

Comment by Stuart: The reference to "Children of the Light" can be traced to verse 50 of *The Gospel of Thomas,* one of the texts in the Nag Hammadi Library although this seems to be a shortened and simplified version. Of course, this striking passage may have been quoted widely in the oral tradition before it became crystallized in a written form.

It is also possible to find echoes here of earlier references in the *Dead Sea Scrolls.* However, this kind of "referring back" was a common practice at that time. The emergent Christian groups also had their favorite sayings from Jeshua. This referencing process was a way of consolidating groups by promoting a sense of inclusiveness.

15. The Journey of the Soul

Alariel: Concerning the Journey of the Soul, Mary Magdalene said this:

> Jeshua spoke often of the journey made by the soul. He spoke of the great longing of the soul for joy and of its descent into the material world so that joy could be experienced intensely. And he told me that the price of this descent was twofold.
>
> First, there would be a separation into male and female, so that from that point onwards, no human being would feel complete in themselves. And secondly, there would be a veiling of awareness, so that human beings would no longer see their own nature with any clarity.
>
> And Jeshua told me that the combination of separation and veiling led to a deep level of confusion, so that many became lost and pursued dreams and shadows instead of Truth. But after many lives living in this shadowy half-world, the soul awakened and ascended again into the Light.
>
> In its ascension, the soul encountered seven great Powers,

symbolizing all the limitations of the human condition. But through the experience of many lives and the knowledge gained upon this path, the soul had become strong. And after answering each one of the Powers in turn, the soul went on its way, rejoicing greatly.

And so at last the soul came to the Gatekeeper, who said, 'Where are you going, Slayer of Human Limitations, Conqueror of all the Realms of Space?'

And the soul answered, 'Through the experience of many lives, I have released myself from all the bondages of this world. I have transcended all roles, set aside the littleness of human life, and now the veil of forgetfulness has fallen from my eyes. At last I can see my real nature as a Child of the Light. Let the clamor of conflict be silent, for I go forth to fulfill my destiny throughout the great reaches of space and time.'

And then the soul passed into the Light, and the world saw it no more.

Commentary by Alariel: *The concept of veiling is a powerful one. Human beings come to the Earth with a veil of forgetting, so that they are not aware of their real nature as great Beings of Light. Once they had agreed at the soul level to experience the full gamut of physical existence, some sort of veiling was necessary for this process to be meaningful.*

Think of it in terms of playing a game. If you begin the game with a full awareness of being a Master of that game, you will not commit yourself fully to the game nor will you learn very much from

114

it. *Your attitude might be, "I've really done all this. It's absurdly simple, so I'll just coast along."*

To extract the maximum learning and growth from playing the game of being human, the Children of the Light did not want just to "coast along"—they wanted all the intensity at the emotional level that comes from a state of uncertainty and incomplete information which forces one to take leaps of faith and trust. To achieve that, there had to be a veiling process, so this is how human life on Earth has been set up.

Don't feel like a victim in this process. At the soul level in the world of Spirit before your first human life, you decided on the rules of this game, and no one imposed them upon you, but it is also you who will decide upon the time of your Awakening when you pull aside the veil and discover who you really are as a multidimensional Being of Light. That is the moment when you step into your spiritual power, and effectively that's the time when this game ends.

Then another game—which we shall call "Ascending into the Light"—begins!

This Magdalene Summary is also remarkable for the way in which it establishes interesting parallels with a passage in The Gospel of Mary, a Gnostic text that has only survived in the modern world in a fragmentary form.

Comment by Stuart: The passage in question runs from pages 16 to 17. Of the eighteen pages of the original text of *The Gospel of Mary,* only eight have survived. The missing ten pages have been recovered through a channeling process and are published in *The Secret Teachings of Mary*

Magdalene by Claire Nahmad and Margaret Bailey. (See the Further Reading section under Nahmad.)

16. The Nature of Salvation

Alariel: Concerning the Nature of Salvation, Mary Magdalene said this:

Salvation—which is the achievement of enlightened consciousness—is often talked of but seldom understood. Those who do not have a clear understanding of the role of the Teacher are particularly prone to confusion. Yet the place of Salvation in our lives may be simply stated:

The Savior saves us from ignorance of The Way,
but we must save ourselves
by continuing to tread The Way
until we merge fully with the Light.

Those who do not see the Teacher clearly may often think that faith in the Teacher alone will save us. It will not! Are we puppets that someone else has to pull our strings and do everything for us? Surely we have a role to play in our own Salvation or else that triumph would be a triumph for the Teacher alone, and we would not deserve the Eternal Joy into which we shall surely rise.

The ignorant may think that Salvation is a one-time thing. The Savior saves us and then all is well forever. These are but the foolish musings of a child. When the Savior opens the door to The Way for us, the work is not over but only just begun. Then we are able to start our conscious journey upwards into the Light, a journey that will demand a total openness to change and transformation on every level of our being.

If there are those who think that you can ascend into the Light taking with you all your old fears and limitations, all your old opinions and prejudices, let them think again. When one who climbs a mountain begins this task, he leaves all his baggage behind to await his return. He must ascend the peak with the minimum of what is necessary, for too much baggage will certainly ensure his failure. So we must become like bold mountain-climbers, shedding everything that is not Light upon our journey to the peak of human achievement.

So Salvation is not a thing of one moment but is continuous. We save ourselves day by day by continuing to climb until our ascension into the Light is completed.

Commentary by Alariel: *Here again Mary returns to the theme of the Savior who "saves us from ignorance of The Way" but then goes on to make a different point about faith in the Teacher. Observe her teaching method here. She clearly knows that this is subtle and abstract information, which some may find difficult to grasp. She responds to this problem with summaries and repetitions, gradually building layer upon layer of ideas until the whole structure of her wisdom becomes clear. And by defining Salvation as the "achievement of enlightened consciousness," she shifts the argument out of the mists of superstition and religion and into a much more psychological and technical framework that you might now associate with the Far Eastern traditions like Hinduism and Buddhism.*

Remember that Jeshua had spent the years from his early teens to the age of thirty traveling along the old Silk Road from Damascus and visiting India and other countries in Asia. The idea of enlightenment would have been strongly established in that region by this point in time, and Jeshua would naturally have absorbed it. As his spiritual partner, Mary Magdalene would have been perfectly placed to absorb these ideas, too, so it is little wonder that they form part of her Summaries.

Comment by Stuart: Even at this very early stage when the ideas of Jeshua were just beginning to go out into the world, Mary has noticed that some people think that faith and faith alone will guarantee their salvation. There was certainly a tendency in the Middle East at that time to overvalue faith and put too much weight upon the idea of a Perfect Teacher who would somehow magically do everything for you. And this idea has proved so durable that even today people travel widely searching for the ideal Teacher, Mentor, or Guru.

Mary contradicts this idea by saying very firmly that we need to make the effort for ourselves—we need to "save ourselves day by day." Bear in mind that Mary was brought up in an Essene tradition with a strong emphasis on individual effort. Here she is putting down a marker which shows she is still building on Essene ideas even if that divides the Gnostics from the followers of the emergent Christian Church.

The other really remarkable thing about this Magdalene Summary is its brevity. Mary makes a comprehensive statement, including a final inspiring summation and then stops. Such is the mastery of compression in her statement that it contains all we need to know about the subject with scarcely a superfluous word. What superb communication this is!

17. The Way

Alariel: Concerning The Way, Mary Magdalene said this:

> The Way is the process through which the Christ Energy transforms your life and your consciousness, and the sign of the Christ Energy working in the heart is the experience of joy. Follow the joy deep within you, for it is a beacon, a sign of Father-Mother God's Truth. Follow this, and it will speak to you and become your guide. When joy sings like a sweet bird in your heart, you know your feet are firmly upon The Way.
>
> There are many practical aspects to the process of treading The Way:
>
> > Firstly, Prayer—not in the sense of asking Father-Mother God for something but rather a laying of your consciousness alongside the consciousness of Father-Mother God, so that the two can resonate together and become one. And also a contemplating of the aspects of the Divine, including the Light, the

Christ Energy, and the All. Let these focus and expand within you and fill your whole being.

Secondly, Forgiveness as a regular evening practice so that all the tangled energies of the day can be brought into Harmony. Through Forgiveness the slate is wiped clean, and we start afresh upon each new day.

Thirdly, Service so that we bring whatever skills we have to address the needs of those we meet. Service is Oneness in action.

Fourthly, Giving Thanks so that we express our gratefulness to Father-Mother God for all the blessings in our life.

Fifthly, Surrender so that the soul can merge with the Light and complete its journey. Find a form of words to express your surrender to the Spirit and repeat this often.

The Way lies in every step you take upon your path until you complete the journey of the soul. Every good thought, every kind word, every helpful deed, every moment of inspiration is part of The Way.

Do not listen to those who try to make a rigid structure of The Way, for they have not understood it. The Way is more valuable to you than any structure. Your salvation lies in the process, not in the structure.

For The Way to live, it must breathe and change like any living thing, so be ready to change and adapt all aspects of it to suit your needs. Though The Way is one, the possibilities of departing from it are many:

If you cling to the books, you've lost The Way.

If you cling to a tradition, you've lost The Way.

If you cling to a ritual, you've lost The Way.

If you cling to the Teacher, you've lost The Way.

The Way is not to be found in books or traditions or rituals or even in the Teacher. The Way is found in treading the path from day to day, guided by your soul and inspired by the Spirit within.

No individual knows the full extent of his or her own path. You can see a little of it, just the track as it curves around the next bend and disappears from sight. Yet that little glimpse is enough. Walk it and see where it will lead, what it will teach, and how it will change you.

The Way is reborn each day as you become open to it and closed to all the opinionated, narrow, judgmental habits of the old world that you are leaving behind.

Those habits are rooted in illusion. Cast them out and follow the Way that opens up before you. Then you will understand the Truth, then you will know Reality, and then you will see things as they really are.

Everything has its roots, its fundamental nature. The Spirit is Light, and we are the Children of the Light. The soul in its journey descends into physical life, passes through the world of form, and wanders among the shadows of illusion like one who is asleep until awakened by the Christ Energy. This is the power of Love arising in the heart.

Awakened by Love, the soul ascends into the Light and merges again with its roots, its essential nature, which is Light. This is the core of what Jeshua taught: we came from the Light; the soul journeys upon the Earth and ascends again into the Light. So Light is our source, our nature, and our goal, but it is the Energy of Love which awakens us and enables us to complete our journey.

When speaking of these things, this is what Jeshua said to me:

This journey is the knowledge I bring you;

this Love is the power of the Christ I awaken in you.

The Christ transforms your life and lifts you up,

and this ascension is the gift I give you.

Listen to the knowledge,
open your heart to the Christ Energy,
transform your life and ascend.
This is The Way:
if you follow this path, you follow me
and will join me in the greater life of Eternal Joy.

This is what Jeshua taught me—this is The Way.

Commentary by Alariel: *Here Mary Magdalene shifts The Way from the realm of theory to the level of everyday experience. She translates it from an idea into a series of practical things that an aspirant can apply in their daily life. In doing so, she combines a firm grasp of advanced ideas with a practical and down-to-earth approach—no wonder the Gnostics valued Mary so highly and revered her as their supreme Teacher!*

Above all, Mary Magdalene was the Bringer of The Way. Jeshua taught The Way, but it was Mary who brought it out into the world and into the lives of all who would listen. Through Mary Magdalene's grace, they were able to see the practical nature of The Way and apply it in their own lives.

The section on prayer is important because it shows Mary using prayer as a form of meditation. That may surprise some people in the West because meditation is now widely seen as essentially an Eastern practice, being associated with Hindus, Buddhists, and Taoists. In fact, meditation was widely used throughout the Middle East at the time of Jeshua, especially in the Mystery Schools. And many of the Essene processes of attunement to angels, for example, were really forms of meditation—they were just not labeled as such.

The importance of Forgiveness was stressed by both Jeshua and Mary Magdalene. Here is a form of words focusing on Forgiveness that circulated amongst some of the Gnostic groups:

> I forgive all the beings who have caused me pain, and I ask those I have hurt to forgive me, also. And I forgive myself, knowing that I carry love for all beings in my heart, and I know that however often I stumble, I never cease my journey to the Light.

And here is a widely used form of words focusing on surrender:

> I surrender to the Spirit.
> I surrender to the Light.
> I am Light.
> I am Light.
> I am Light.

At its deepest level, The Way is about the journey home:

> Home out of the shadows and the illusions,
> Home out of limitation and littleness,
> Home into the Light.

Compared to this process—the journey of the soul—no knowledge or doctrine or tradition really matters. Everything else you do upon planet Earth is only a prelude to this final triumph—the return into Oneness of every soul, every single Child of the

Light. For this is the Conscious Realization of the All, the coming together of the fragments in the Wholeness of the One.

Comment by Stuart: How is it that Mary Magdalene's five points summarizing The Way can seem both familiar and yet also strikingly new? Has Mary found some connecting thread in Jeshua's teachings which reveals a coherent structure that other teachers have missed? And given their common source of inspiration in Jeshua, how is it that Mary and the early Church Fathers should have reached such different conclusions? There is certainly no denying the profound differences here. While Christianity is a religion, Mary's account of The Way reveals it to be a spiritual path that needs no hierarchies or doctrines to sustain it.

And that's not the only surprise here. When Mary talks about prayer, she lifts that idea out of the realm of ceremony and ritual and into a very modern framework of meditation and contemplation.

When Mary says, "If you cling to the books, you've lost the way," this sends a powerful signal to our overly intellectual society. The great American architect Frank Lloyd Wright echoes this idea when he says:

> Read the books and throw the books away because it's not in the books, but there it is: out in the fields, in the trees, in the nature of things.

Though Mary's five-point presentation may seem a new process, it actually has very ancient roots. Teachers working within an oral tradition would often try to find clusters of points that they could gather together in fives or tens because then they could tick off these points on the fingers of one or two hands.

How powerful the emphasis here is upon process rather than doctrine or structure. And how different from the emergent Christian Church which started to build structures from the very beginning: priests, bishops, and archbishops; doctrines, rituals, and credos. Here Mary Magdalene is saying that structure is secondary. What will get you to salvation is the process of The Way. And this is essentially your *individual* spiritual path—the application of these principles in your own life and your own experience. This shifts the spiritual process from an organization-centered approach to a much more democratic basis where the individual is in charge of his/her own destiny.

18. Balance and Harmony

Alariel: Concerning Balance and Harmony, Mary Magdalene said this:

> The Universe moves constantly towards Harmony and is sustained by a system of balances. When you know about these balances you begin to understand the true nature of things. In this way an understanding of balance helps you to penetrate the veil of illusion and see things as they really are.
>
> Throughout creation there are a series of spectrums of Energy with opposing polarities that seem to be at war with one another. Yet this is an illusion, for at the Midway Point within each spectrum, the extremes vanish and all is brought into equilibrium. Opposites are identical in nature but different in frequency. Thus hot and cold are identical in their essential nature, which is one of temperature, but they represent different frequencies within that spectrum.
>
> Human life seems to be full of these pairs of opposites, including gain and loss, activity and stillness, more and less, loving and hating, greater and lesser, and these

dualities do seem to dominate your lives. Consider, for example, the duality of gain and loss. This spectrum of Energy is about supply: gain is a plus of supply and loss is a minus of it. Only on one point in the spectrum—the Midway Point—is it in balance. Here there is no gain and no loss, just the Harmony and oneness of supply. If you reject and push away any of the energies on this spectrum or try to attract and draw to you any of these energies, then you are not at the Midway Point.

Try to focus and live at the Midway Point on all the spectrums of Energy: at this point there is a resolution of all energies. Here there is balance, here there is equilibrium, and here there is peace. Here there is direct knowledge of Reality, for at any other point on the spectrum—plus or minus—you will be influenced by the illusion that one end of the spectrum is better than the other end, and you will not be able to see things as they really are.

Once you know about this system of duality, your perception of gain and loss shifts onto a more subtle level, and you begin to ask yourself more fundamental questions:

- Is a gain only an apparent gain?
- Is a loss only an apparent loss?
- Could a loss on the physical level really be something quite different if it led to a gain on the spiritual level?
- And is the whole spectrum of

gain and loss not about acquiring and losing at all but about seeing into the real nature of things and looking beyond duality into the Oneness of the Real?

Learn to look at all the dualities in life as linked together within these spectrums of Energy. Focus on the Midway Point and bring the opposites together in your consciousness, affirming that what you are seeing is not duality at all but the fundamental transcendent Oneness of things. In this state of non-duality, you become increasingly sensitive and aware of the Reality which is the All. And the more you integrate with non-duality, the more the illusions dissolve, and the veil of forgetting begins to thin. Here at last you can begin to see things as they really are and start to understand your own true nature as a Being of Light.

All this greatly increases your sensitivity to balance and Harmony. These are keys to the process of spiritual unfoldment, so be aware of the effect your behavior has upon your inner balance. Arguing for this or denying that removes Harmony from your consciousness. By accepting everything that happens to you as part of the balance of Father-Mother God's Creation, you affirm Harmony.

Through Harmony
the Universe moves back into its
natural state,
and the All sings within the silence
of the heart.

Commentary by Alariel: *This Summary reveals the advanced and subtle nature of Mary Magdalene's consciousness. While Peter was "fighting the good fight," Mary soared up into non-duality and the transcendent state of the Real. The Church did not teach anything about the nature of Reality; indeed, it suppressed all knowledge of this kind, regarding it at best as an unwelcome diversion from the task of saving souls and at worst something even more sinister—a way of undermining Church authority.*

The pairs of opposites may seem a very strange concept to the Western mind, but these ideas already exist in Western tradition. The great Sage known to the Greeks as Hermes and to the Egyptians as Thoth used opposites as a central element in his teaching, calling this the "Principle of Polarity." Unfortunately, this information—well-known to the Mystery Schools—never percolated through the mainstream of Western thought, and so most people in the West were not able to benefit from deeper knowledge of this kind.

This deeper knowledge will help you to understand the importance of balance at every level of the Universe and why Harmony is such a supreme and fundamental law. To enter conflict—even in a just cause—is to turn your back on Harmony and move away from the nature of Reality. Become sensitive to every little ripple of disharmony in your life. Resolve it and ask Forgiveness of any you may have wronged. Use a constant process of

Forgiveness to deal with the ripples of disharmony, so that they never develop into waves that threaten your inner peace.

Comment by Stuart: There is such depth to this teaching on non-duality! Consider for a moment one duality that has caused much suffering within the Essene soul family: the duality of Giving and Receiving. In the words of St. Ignatius Loyola in his "Prayer for Generosity," over the last 2,000 years we have become so focused on the need "to give and not to count the cost" that, in effect, we have shut down our ability to receive. Is this why so many Lightworkers seem to have Abundance issues?

The idea that you are in illusion at either end of a spectrum of Energy but can have direct knowledge of Reality at the Midway Point is highly significant. We may all know people who take a simplistic black-and-white view of the world, and now we can see what is going on with them. Because they focus on extreme positions, they simply can't see things as they really are because they are blinded by the illusion that dominates any extreme point. It is no use trying to reason with people like this. Because of the power of the Energy at the extreme point, they will sincerely believe they are right—even when they are absurdly wrong.

At this point I still felt we needed more insight on how duality affects our lives, so I went back to Alariel for more information.

Alariel: While you remain within the third dimensional realm, the dualities of gain and loss/better and worse will continue to be important in your lives. Although it is beneficial to focus on the *ideal* of Oneness, the final achievement of an enduring state of Oneness has to come when you are ready for it.

People who think it is easy to enter complete Oneness—and live permanently on that level—have underestimated the amount of self-work that is required to deal with the agenda of emotional issues, 'story,' and cellular memories. Full entry into a state of non-duality and the permanent merging with Oneness is an advanced state of human development and should be recognized as such.

19. Truth and Freedom

Alariel: Concerning Truth and Freedom, Mary Magdalene said this:

> You either want to find the Truth of things, or you do not. If you are dedicated to the Light, to the Truth, you will let everything else go until you find it. And even if the Truth is difficult and challenging at times, you will keep on treading this path until you reach the Light. Because when you know the Truth, it sets you free from all the illusions of this world. Standing within the Truth, you can see things as they really are, and you can understand the nature of the All.
>
> The All is not dual in its nature; it is not fragmented or not divided because it is entirely focused on Oneness. To illustrate this, let us take the example of a wise man—we shall call him Joseph—who raises his consciousness to the level of the All and fully enters Reality. What will he find there?
>
> In the Real he will find no person, no thing, no concept, no space, and no time, but what IS there is Supreme Consciousness. When Joseph enters the

Real, his *'Josephness'* disappears, and he becomes pure awareness—the Supreme Consciousness. And if you joined him there, your existence as a separate being would vanish, too, and your consciousness and the consciousness-that-had-once-been-Joseph would not be two 'consciousnesses' but *one* Consciousness. And if all the sentient Beings of all the Universes also entered the Real, there would still be only one Consciousness. For at that level only Oneness exists, and all separateness falls away like the sands of the desert blowing away upon the wind.

When there is no longer a 'you' and an 'I,' this may seem like emptiness, but there is a deep mystery here. The All, which seems to contain nothing, actually contains everything—but at the level of pure and unified consciousness—not at the lower level of separation and illusion. The many that seem to exist do not really exist. They are just projections like a picture painted with Energy, not the solid Reality that they seem to be. And at the highest level of Consciousness, there is only One—only the All.

In the awareness of that Oneness lies a direct pathway to the Light. This is the secret knowledge that can liberate you from the veils of illusion and the chains of powerlessness. This knowledge of non-duality connects you with your real nature as a Child of the Light, empowering you to step forward and claim your Divine Heritage. You have been living in a world of dreams, of illusion. Now it is time to wake up and step into Reality and begin to understand the All.

The world of illusion was appropriate for you when you were spiritual children, but when you seek to know the Truth and enter Reality, you begin to function as spiritual adults. The Truth may not always be easy, and it may not always be comfortable, but it dissolves the limitations that bind you. Above all, it is the Truth that liberates you from your littleness and shows you the great Beings of Light that you really are. This is the way you can tell if it is the real Truth, for the Truth sets you free.

> Dreams confuse,
> illusions bind,
> but the Truth always sets you free.

Comment by Stuart: The best-known quotation on this subject comes from John's Gospel, chapter 8, verse 31: "If you hold to my teaching, you are really my disciples; you will know the truth and the truth will set you free."

Commentary by Alariel: *This passage has become distorted over time. The original version reads like this: 'If you follow The Way that I have taught you, you are really my disciples: by treading the path you will find the Truth, and the Truth will set you free.'*

This Magdalene Summary underlines the whole point of Mary Magdalene's teachings. She is not saying all this to play with interesting ideas. The point of knowing about Reality is that it can set you

*free!   You can step out of your limitations, your
addictions, your confusion, and your fear, and rise
into a higher state of consciousness that will give you
access to empowerment, and even as the Dead Sea
Scrolls put it 'Eternal joy in life without end.'*

*There are a thousand illusions but only one
Reality, only one Truth.   When you step out of
illusion and enter Reality, the Truth you see is
exactly the same Truth that every enlightened being
has seen since the beginning of time.*

*There are two key aspects of Truth: Truth
about yourself and Truth about the nature of Reality.
And these aspects of Truth lead to a transcendent
understanding that your inner Self and Reality are
not two things—but One Thing! This is the Truth that
can set you free from the Great Illusion of
Separateness and liberate you from the domination
of the ego by opening a pathway to the Light.*

Comment by Stuart: It is certainly true that the
Gnostics—the knowers of the Truth—were far more
interested in liberation than in spending years
locked into a study of complex doctrine. Doctrinal
dictatorship was exactly the opposite of what the
Gnostics stood for, but perhaps it was their acute
intelligence that sealed their fate: they stood for the
kind of intellectually-based spiritual democracy
that the Church most feared and hated. Because
once a Gnostic had freed himself by becoming a
knower of the Truth, he would never need a bishop
to tell him what the Truth was!

20. Oneness and the All

Alariel: Concerning Oneness and the All, Mary Magdalene said this:

Many people in the early stages of thinking about Oneness see only the smooth and comfortable side of it, but as you journey to the core of Oneness, you will discover many layers of challenge. Looking beyond every kind of duality and living at the Midway Point of balance is only the beginning of it.

As the All values every culture, every race, and every tradition equally, you will have to throw away all your prejudices and opinions and live in an opinion-less state.

The All teaches you to accept everything that happens to you with an open mind and an open heart, and it teaches you to live in the present moment and let go of all of the past—your tradition's past, your teacher's past, your country's past, even your own past. When you live completely in the All, you rise up each morning like a newborn babe greeting a fresh day: nothing in your consciousness is fixed, and all of your consciousness is open to whatever the Universe has to teach you.

Then you will cease to seek teachers only amongst human beings or angels, realizing that any little creature, any flower, or any beautiful aspect of landscape or sky can teach you profound lessons as you tread your path. And in time you will come to value the everyday experiences of your daily life as your very best teachers.

When you live in the harmony of the All, you are the friend of everyone and the enemy of no one. Even time will expand and contract to serve you, and you will begin to observe Father-Mother God in everything you see. Seeing Father-Mother God in everyone and everything that you encounter will change your perception of the sacred, and you will begin to find wisdom and perfection everywhere, even in apparent folly and chaos. If you should travel through a land in conflict, you will see only peace, and your presence will bless everyone you meet, for it will remind them of their own peace that comes from within. Rooted in the Real, you will bring a glimpse of Reality into every life you touch.

Because the All contains all space and all time, it also transcends all space and all time. By attuning to the Real, all knowledge and all wisdom can be accessed. But accessing knowledge and wisdom is one thing, and being able to absorb and apply it is another. When the consciousness reaches a certain level, the wisdom of that level becomes available to you, and you are able to retain it and use it because you are on the appropriate level to do so. If you access a level of wisdom beyond your level of consciousness, it will be slippery, like a fish, and will slide out of your mind before you can absorb and apply it.

The most important thing you can say about the All is that it is not dual in nature. In a non-dual state, all judgments are transcended in a consciousness that rises up to see the Oneness that exists beyond the illusion of duality. When you rise in consciousness and see the bigger picture, all the warring duality of this world seems like a sham, a distorted dream that has no roots in the Real. In that Reality, what exists is one Essence, one Supreme Consciousness. When you realize that you are of the same Essence as the greatest Archangel, you begin to sense your true nature as a Child of the Light. And when you begin to understand that all is Light, all is Spirit, your consciousness starts to change. Then you begin to see the Essence of Father-Mother God moving out across the Universe in great waves of life and growth and expanding consciousness. Then you can see how life can change, moving up through all the kingdoms so that consciousness moves slowly as a rock, quickens as a plant, awakens as an animal, and when a human soul is created, expands into the faster rhythm and deeper awareness of human life. Then you will know that all living things are your brothers and sisters, and all life contains the Essence of Father-Mother God.

From this understanding, certain Principles emerge:

1. Only Father-Mother God exists: everything and every being in the Universe contains the Divine Essence;
2. That Essence exists at first only in potential, and it is realized through the expansion of consciousness;
3. The Divine Essence moves in waves of creation through all the kingdoms of life, culminating in the human kingdom;
4. On planetary systems where there is free will, beings may choose for a time to move away from the Light;
5. There is no sin, only a moving away from Father-Mother God and a returning to the Divine;
6. The journey of the soul upon Earth is a process of learning and growing, an opportunity to respond to Love and experience Joy;
7. The Universe is a vast Web of integrated Beingness, unified by Energy and linked by Consciousness. So all are within

the One, and the One is present within all life forms.

When you first encounter the All, it may seem like a vast Emptiness. Do not be deceived into thinking there is nothing there! No form exists there, no image, no idea, no *thing,* but there is a Supreme and Unifying Consciousness. Because this Supreme Consciousness is the same for you and me and any being, it is essentially One and is not divided. Your lower awareness may perceive this Supreme Consciousness as placed within many beings, many forms, but that individual awareness is looking at the All from the standpoint of illusion. In Truth, there is no separation, no division, no *'manyness'* —only Oneness of Consciousness in which you and all other beings share equally.

Nothing in the All can ever be threatened or diminished, for if you took away something from the All, there would be the All and something-that-has-been-taken-away. This would be duality and duality is the Great Illusion. Ignore the many faces of illusion and live serenely in the All.

Behold, your individual ascension is part of the ascension of the Earth, and the Earth's ascension is part of the ascension of the Universe, and the Universe's ascension is part of the ascension of the All. But although the time to speak of the Ascension of the All has not yet come, each soul ascending into the Light brings forward the day when the seals will be opened, and the Truth of this ultimate Ascension will be given.

> So go forward with courage into the Light,
> knowing that you are part of a Divine Plan
> vaster than any human mind can imagine
> and more full of Joy
> than any human heart can understand.

Commentary by Alariel: *Here Mary reveals the full majestic sweep of her philosophy. But notice how controversial this is: the idea that all things and beings in the Universe contain God is certainly Pantheism, a perception that was denounced by the Church as heresy. Yet such is the gentle power and wise authority of Mary Magdalene that these Magdalene Summaries can be accepted as the deep and transcendent truth of things—a truth that makes much more sense and leads to a much greater understanding of life than the simplistic version presented by the Church.*

Comment by Stuart: Mary only uses the word "Behold" once in all these Magdalene Summaries, so we know that here she is about to reveal information of the highest level and the greatest significance. This is Mary Magdalene as Prophet and Seer, gazing into future time and bringing back a clear vision to inspire and guide us. So intense is the drama at this point at the very end of this last Magdalene Summary that we can almost sense those who heard her being spurred into a more intense level of concentration. For here she projects way into the future and relates that future to the process of individual ascension.

However dramatic that may have been when Mary spoke these words 2,000 years ago, the present situation gives it an even sharper relevance. For we have reached a point at the end of the planetary cycle when Transition for both individual human beings and planet Earth is imminent. And at this point we are taking a big step forward towards this ultimate goal of the whole Creation—the Ascension of the All. (The Ascension of the All is mentioned in the Gnostic text called *Pistis Sophia,* on page 433 in the Hurtak translation.)

The session with Alariel continues.

Alariel: It may seem strange to present the human kingdom as the 'culminating' factor of all the waves of Creation, especially now that humanity is struggling with so much illusion and chaos. But the truth is that from this point on, the whole arc of your spiritual development will stay within the human kingdom *as a broad category of classification,* however advanced and subtle your consciousness may become. The really big shifts are those from rock to plant, plant to animal, and animal to human—and 'kingdom' is, therefore, a good description of those major stages.

Comment by Stuart: Now we can see these Magdalene Summaries as a whole. We can assess where they stand, and one thing becomes instantly clear: we are entering new territory in these Magdalene Summaries. This isn't Christianity. This is not religion of any kind; it is something quite different—something that the poet Tagore once called "the allness of the universe."

This is pure Mystery School teaching with Light as the central symbol. And the key here is the source of the teaching. At one point Mary advises her listeners to be "Open to whatever the Universe has to teach you." For the emergent Christian Church, the teaching is done by the Church, the priest, the scripture. But for Mary it is the Universe—and a combination of the Earthly Mother and the Heavenly Father can, indeed, be perceived as the Universe!

See how true Mary was to her Essene roots but notice also how she built upon this foundation, and drawing upon her training as a High Priestess of Isis, she was able to lift this teaching up to a higher level. Here you are seeing the elements within Essene philosophy being transmuted into a higher, simpler, and more universal wisdom. This is Mary Magdalene as alchemist, lifting up the Essene impulse into the highest level of Gnostic achievement.

21. Key Questions and Answers

Alariel: Throughout the eight Midsummer Gatherings, a few key themes kept recurring. We have chosen a selection of questions that were asked at that time in order to highlight these themes.

What is the biggest challenge facing us?
Mary Magdalene: Keeping The Way simple. Jeshua taught us a simple path, but simplicity will not appeal to everyone, and many may succumb to the temptation to 'improve' upon The Way by elaborating and embellishing it. That temptation should always be resisted!

What is the greatest enemy of those who follow The Way?
Mary Magdalene: Fear. There will be times upon this path when it may seem that the whole world is against us. Do not listen to this voice of fear within, for it comes from a distorted view of Reality. In Truth, we are stronger than all the armies of fear, for instead of fighting hatred with hatred, we fill our hearts and minds with the strongest power in all the world—the power

of Universal Love. Love does not fight or seek for conquest or dominion. Instead of cursing, Love blesses all who touch it and raises up even those who would try to bring you down. When you serve Love, you walk with your hands in the hands of angels, knowing that nothing can prevent the ultimate Triumph of the Light.

Jeshua talked about "Empty-Fullness." Could you explain this, please?

Mary Magdalene: When he talked about the state of Empty-Fullness, he was advising us to become empty of the little selfish lower self and rise up and become full of the Spirit. For when you are full of the Spirit, you enter your own true nature, all limitations fall away from you, and all things become possible.

How can we attune to the Kingdom of Heaven?

Mary Magdalene: The Kingdom is within you, and in all the Universe outside you, and you will reach a point where you realize that the Universe outside and the Self within are *One* and are not divided. This is the beginning of wisdom. Then you will know that you are a Child of the Light and you *are* Light, and you will also know that nothing in the realm of Spirit can ever be threatened or diminished.

The Savior did such wonderful things that many are now saying that he must be God. You were closer to him than any of us. What do you say?

Mary Magdalene: In the Jewish tradition, the Messiah is seen as a great Prophet and the Savior of his people but not as God. Indeed, our tradition forbids us from talking about any man as if he was God. Remember what Jeshua said, 'All that I do, you will someday be able to do and even greater things than these.' This is our guarantee that Jeshua is just as each human being is—a Child of the Light. If Jeshua was the Son of God, that saying would be meaningless. How can any human being hope to do as the Son of God does and more also? You can worship a Son of God, but you cannot follow in his footsteps, and Jeshua asked us to do exactly that.

Comment by Stuart: See how neatly Mary answers this question, rooting her answer in the Judaic tradition and quoting directly from Jeshua. It is quite clear where Mary stands on this issue, but her answer is based upon reason and not on her own personal opinion.

There is no doubt that this is one of the areas of major controversy within Christianity with this statement by Jeshua contradicting the conventional view of the Trinity. This is clearly one of the key sayings of Jeshua and would have been circulated orally before appearing in any written form. We know it as part of the Gospel of John, chapter 14: 12. There is a direct conflict here: it does not seem possible to reconcile the idea of Only Sonship with the statement that we will one day be able to do all that Jeshua has done.

It is worth noting in this context that the Christians of the first century did not believe that Jesus was the Only Son of God—that perception became part of doctrine much later in Christian history. Argument on this issue raged throughout the Christian world in the first two centuries of the Christian era, and it was only after the adoption of the Nicene Creed in 325 CE that most Christians accepted the new concept. That did not stop some theologians from opposing this idea for the remainder of the fourth century, and even today there are theologians who dispute the idea of "eternal sonship."

The channeling from Alariel continues.

The Zealots are saying that he did not save us because the Romans are still in our land.
Mary Magdalene: Jeshua fulfilled the prophecy. He did save his people Israel, but at the spiritual level. Our religion is old now and has grown inward-looking and over-ritualistic. He opened up the windows of the soul and showed us a better way to live, a Way that leads directly to the Light. His Kingdom is not of this world, and that is why the Romans are not his concern.

What is the biggest mistake we can make on the spiritual path?
Mary Magdalene: To see yourself as small and powerless: the truth is that you are vast, powerful, and loving Beings of Light. You have been struggling here on Earth so long that you have forgotten who you really are.

You think you are weak and limited and bound, but in truth you are powerful and free. And as you follow The Way, all boundaries will fall away from you, and you will mount up on wings of Spirit like eagles and soar up into the everlasting Joy of the Ascended Realm of Being.

How will the experience of Oneness change us?

Mary Magdalene: All things will be in you, and you will be in all. The smallest bird will sing your song, and the greatest angel will be your friend. The rivers will run deep within you, and you will feel the movement of the ocean. The planets will be your companions, and you will be one with all the energies of the stars.

How many lives have you had upon the Earth?

Mary Magdalene: Like most human beings, I have had many hundreds of Earth-lives. There are exceptions to this general pattern—sometimes you will meet an angel for whom this is the first and perhaps the only human experience, and sometimes beings come here for one or two lives from their homes in far-distant places amongst the stars. But the number of angels and star-beings on Earth at present is tiny, like a few grains of sand in a desert. All the rest—all the great mass of humanity—will have many lives here. And some of these lives become especially precious to us. I had a life as a poet in Persia, which is one of my happiest memories, which is why I chose to have a Persian grandfather—these things are arranged by the angels long before we set foot upon the Earth.

Comment by Stuart: The reference to Persia is fascinating. Thanks to Alariel we already knew that Mary Magdalene's grandfather was Balthazar, but we had no idea why there would be this Persian connection. It is certainly true that many of Mary's teachings have a poetic rhythm and intensity about them, and perhaps this will help us to understand why this should be. We have no idea who this Persian poet might be and would be interested in feedback from any reader who is more expert in this area than we are. Alariel is resisting giving us any more information here, explaining it in this way:

Alariel: Research into this area should prove an interesting project for any who wish to follow it up! This underlines how much of a team effort all this is. Think of it as a Rainbow Tapestry of Truth—every human being bringing his/her own perceptions to make up the Rainbow of human consciousness. There was a time when Truth was perceived by the few and handed down to the many. Now humanity has reached a stage where every man, woman, and child can contribute to the totality of Truth.

Comment by Stuart: This phrase the "Rainbow Tapestry of Truth" first emerged during an email correspondence with William Brune of Missouri.

The channeling from Alariel continues:

What is the most under-valued aspect of the spiritual path?

Mary Magdalene: The Brotherhood of Angels and of Men. Try to attune constantly to the innocence of angels. Then you will wake up one morning and look out of your eyes as the Angel That You Are. All your senses will have moved up into a new frequency, and you will enter a new world as a Spiritual Angel—a reborn Child of the Light.

Where is the Kingdom of Heaven?

Mary Magdalene: The Kingdom of Heaven is everywhere—in the Universe all round you and in the innermost temple of your heart. If you do not know the Kingdom of Heaven, you will live in poverty even though you have riches beyond all the dreams of men because you will constantly suspect the thief and fear the assassin, and you will never be able to enjoy your wealth. But when you know the Kingdom of Heaven, all the Abundance of the Universe is spread out before you, all the birds sing to celebrate your passing, and every day brings the blessing of countless angels on your path.

Then you will walk a path of Harmony and peace, and you will know the joy of service, which is perfect freedom. For when you never consider yourself and always consider those around you, you will have no time for doubt or worry, and every moment of your waking consciousness will be filled with the radiance of true happiness. Then no burden will seem too heavy and no path too steep, for you will journey always in the company of friends, and your focus will be upon the Kingdom of Heaven, which is Love and Laughter and everlasting Joy.

Alariel: John was always present at the Gatherings, asking profound and thoughtful questions like these.

John: *What image should we focus on to sum up the progress of humanity towards the Light?*

Mary Magdalene: Humanity has been plodding along like a weary man carrying a heavy burden of deep sorrow, yet now you shall become like a sweet bird, soaring up into the blue horizon of endless joy. The time for suffering and all forms of heaviness is over. Let the lightness of the Spirit fill your hearts and lift you into a better world where you shall live as fully conscious Children of the Light and walk with your hands in the hands of angels. Jeshua, who had tasted all the sweetness of eternal joy, felt deep compassion for the sufferings of poor blind humanity. That is why he taught so simple a way to joy and Light, so that all might follow him and experience their birthright as Children of the Light.

John: *Sometimes when we talked with Jeshua I could see him reach out with the mind of a Seer and catch the image of a great sweep of Creation moving through all the kingdoms of life. Tell us of your understanding of this.*

Mary Magdalene: Remember that Jeshua had travelled to the East and met great Sages of which our tradition has no knowledge, and from these Great Masters of Wisdom, he learned much—some of which he communicated to me, but not all. He spoke of a vast process of life beginning at the simplest level as rocks and moving through all the kingdoms of life until a human soul was born. And beyond that, he spoke of experience at the human level and of men and women rising into ascended levels of being, but he told me that in many ways, this was only the start of our real education in the Universe . . .

For beyond the ascended level, he spoke of eons of experience as Masters of Knowledge and Travelers upon the Higher Planes of Being, of lives in which we shall be lords of planets and of galaxies until we take our place beside the Elohim, the Great Architects of all the Universal Life. And he spoke of Wisdom without end and Joy beyond our remotest imaginings, of Life more subtle and intense than any human mind could understand, and Love more powerful than any human heart could encompass. And he said that when we understood the full nature of our consciousness, we would know that all we have encountered on this planet was only a prelude, only a beginning . . .

John: *And Jeshua used to say that each planet and star had its own pattern of development, although this was played out over vast reaches of time . . .*

Mary Magdalene: Yes, it is difficult to grasp the scale of time in the life of planets and stars. Jeshua told me that in a few centuries from now, the whole of the Heavens would reach a critical point when the pattern would change. So far, the galaxies have moved out into separation and down into denser physical reality, but when the turning point is reached, all that will change. Then all of Creation will begin to move back into Oneness, back again into Light. And Jeshua said that his work fits within this greater framework, for as our planet moves into Light, so humanity will move back into Oneness and Light also, and we are the early pioneers in this process. Where we go in ones and twos, soon many others will follow, and the path that now seems strange and difficult will become a well-worn highway in which all can share. For though Jeshua seemed sometimes to teach in riddles, that was because the nature of Reality is so little understood now. So few humans have reached the Kingdom of Heaven that it still seems a strange and alien place to most people, but as more and more seekers come to know the Truth, those who teach that Truth will find their words much more widely accepted.

John: *I feel strongly that Jeshua has been my Teacher for many lives—sometimes I understood what he was trying to teach and sometimes sadly I did not. Do you share this feeling?*

Mary   Magdalene: Of course! Nothing is as accidental and haphazard as it seems to be, and the angels are constantly working to bring all the members of our soul group together whenever our Teacher incarnates upon the Earth—and particularly when there is a lifetime as important as this one. In many ways this is the culmination of all the lives in which Jeshua—using many names and wearing many faces—has taught our group. We have all sat at his feet and been inspired by his words, and now at this crucial time for humanity, he has taken the human experience to a new level.

Now he has shown us a Way that is so simple that anyone can follow it and so profound that even the most advanced will discover deep wisdom through treading this path. This path cuts through all the complexity of the past, so that it is a direct route to the Light. It leads to the very peak of achievement of the Mysteries without all the complexity of the ancient Mystery Schools. Jeshua saw that the Mystery School tradition—wonderful though it is—can only be mastered by a few dedicated Initiates. He wanted to open this narrow path and make a broad high road that would take the great mass of humanity to the Light.

The years of detailed esoteric study, of ritual and meditation, are now replaced by a simple path focusing the Energy of Universal Love through the vortex of the heart. Here the same results can be obtained as in the greatest Temples of the Old Tradition. The Energy of Universal Love is so powerful that it can cut through all the obstacles and open a direct route into a transcendent experience of Reality. As one trained in the Ancient Mysteries of Isis, I saw the boldness, the audacity of what he was proposing. If we succeed now, if The Way flourishes, the numbers of enlightened ones will not be mere hundreds as in the past, but thousands, maybe even millions. Is that not a noble cause? Is that not a worthy vehicle for our love, our dedication, and our service?

John: *And is The Way entirely new?*

Mary Magdalene: Yes, entirely. Components of it may be found in many wisdom traditions, but it was the genius of Jeshua to put it together into one integrated whole and present that whole simply and directly.

John: *Jeshua said that if we follow The Way, we would not die. This sounds a bold claim indeed . . .*

Mary Magdalene: The combination of life and death exists when you choose to live as a separate being, focusing on the difference that separates you from the Universe around you. When you follow The Way and rise in wisdom, you will realize that all is One Consciousness, so that you and the Universe are linked into the Greater Oneness of a vast Web of Energy and Being. And then you will become the conqueror of death and the slayer of every human limitation, and you will take your place as an Immortal and Loving Child of the Light.

And when enough human beings have gone through this great change, men will walk with angels, and a time of peace and joy will come to the Earth. Then every man will be your friend, every day will be a new song, and all will work together in Harmony for the greater good.

Comment by Stuart: What I love most of all about the teachings of Mary Magdalene is how she soars up into statements that are full of a unique combination of positivity and poetry. This combination seems to be a hallmark of Mary's teaching, and in it you can see her brilliant mind and her compassionate heart soaring up into new possibilities - and taking her audience into realms that they had never even dreamed of. How could you NOT love a teacher like that?

22. Parallels with
The Gospel of Thomas

Alariel: Many of the questions that arose during the Midsummer Gatherings related to themes that are echoed in the key Gnostic text, *The Gospel of Thomas.* We have gathered together examples of these questions in order to present them here.

Comment by Stuart: I have placed these questions in the order in which the references appear in *The Gospel of Thomas.*

What is the greatest barrier to entering the Kingdom of Heaven?
Mary Magdalene: Anyone who separates the inner world from the outer so that in his/her mind the two never meet—that is the greatest barrier to entering the realms of Light. For if any separate inner and outer, they have not understood the nature of Reality. In the Real, all the Universe is One Thing, and inner and outer, self and other, merge into the transcendent Oneness.
(Note: See verse 22 of *The Gospel of Thomas.* I recommend the fine modern translation in *Beyond*

161

Belief: The Secret Gospel of Thomas by Elaine Pagels.)

What moved Jeshua most and brought out his compassion?

Mary Magdalene: His soul ached for the plight of human beings.   He saw that they were blind in their hearts and could not see what was real.   For consider what the angels can see: they see the whole realm of spirit beings, the flow of energies, and all the subtle workings of the Universe, and deep within each angel there is a song praising the love and beauty of Father-Mother God.   But most men can see none of this.   They see work and drudgery and pain, with no sign of hope anywhere.   They are locked into the heaviness of the world, and the realms of Spirit are invisible to them.   Their eyes may function, but their hearts are blind, and that is what stirred the compassion of Jeshua.   That is why he strove so tirelessly to show us The Way to the Light, so that our hearts could see, and the Spirit within us could rise up singing. For now most men dwell in the poverty of the spirit, and Jeshua, who is full of the Abundance of the Spirit, came to share this abundance with all who are open to receive it.

(Note: See verse 28 of *The Gospel of Thomas*.)

Who will try to rob us of the simplicity of The Way?

Mary Magdalene: Those Pharisees who swim in complexity as fish swim in water and the scholars who take wisdom and wrap it up in the elaborate folds of knowledge, so that it is securely hidden—these are the thieves who will try to rob you of the great gift of the Simple Path. But Jeshua came to break the seals of secrecy and open The Way for all to follow. Follow it in wisdom and in innocence and let your hearts be as light and joyful as the spirits of angels. And when the fearful ones cluster around you and tell you to protect yourself with all their labyrinthine knowledge, laugh at them and leave them to their complexity, for they are making a snare for their own feet and a trap for their own minds. Travel on in innocence and simplicity. That is the path of angels, and it leads directly to the Light. This path of Love needs no defense, and its wisdom needs no explanation, for it flows from the very heart of the Universe.

(Note: See verse 39 of *The Gospel of Thomas*.)

How can we distinguish Light from darkness?

Mary Magdalene: Whoever is undivided - he who recognizes that the Universe and the Self within are One—will be full of Light, but those who are divided, see rivals and enemies everywhere because they are full of darkness. Seek out those who are light and of the Light, those for whom life is a song and a dance, a thing of wisdom and kindness and joy, for these are the friends of angels, and they will lead you to the Light.

(Note: See verse 61 of *The Gospel of Thomas*.)

Will The Way test us and challenge us?

Mary Magdalene: Remember that Jeshua said, 'Whoever is near me is near the fire!' All great spiritual Teachers are like a mirror in which you see yourself, both your virtues and your faults. To be close to a great spiritual Teacher is to approach the transformative fire in which all that is NOT Light within you will be consumed. When all this dross is burned away, what remains is the clarity of the Light within. That is the great gift that the Teacher brings you.

(Note: See verse 82 of *The Gospel of Thomas*.)

Great Sages are said to be able to move mountains. How are they able to do this?

Mary Magdalene: Any physical Reality can be created by those who have fused together the world around us and the Self within, the inner heart with the outer Universe. When these two become One, you have all the power of the Universe at your disposal, but because you will by then have become aligned with the Light, you will not abuse this power. If you have perfect faith that a mountain will move and not even the tiniest shred of doubt about this remains in your consciousness, then the mountain *will* move. For when you know your true Self as a Being of Light, all the potential of the Light stands ready to serve you, as you will stand ready to serve all those who suffer or are in need. Then time and space are set aside, and you create a Reality as Father-Mother God creates—easily and in a single moment.

(Note: See verse 106 of *The Gospel of Thomas.* Mary is speaking here about the process of Instantaneous Creation, an advanced level of Reality creation that is described in chapter 16 of our third book, *Beyond Limitations: The Power of Conscious Co-Creation.*)

Alariel: The disciple Philip, who played a prominent role in all of the Gatherings, asked deep questions, too.

Philip: *Mary, there is one thing that Jeshua said that I have never understood: he said he would guide you and make you male, so that you would become a living spirit and enter the Kingdom of Heaven. What did he mean by this?*

Mary Magdalene: Jeshua said that he would help me follow The Way and unite with the Spirit that is within. For when the lower self and the living Spirit combine, all aspects of gender are transcended and a woman has the same potential as a man. Now we are separated and divided, but when we go forward into the Light, we ascend as Children of the Light beyond all the limitations of form and go forward into that Light together.

(Note: This passage clarifies and explains one of the most baffling and obscure parts of *The Gospel of Thomas* - verse 114.)

Philip: *And must we move beyond form entirely to become one with the Light?*

Mary Magdalene: At the highest level, yes, for Light

and form occupy two different levels of creation, and Light is the higher—so high in vibration that no form can exist within its essence. Though a physical body may be seen as a projection of Light and a soul body as a higher projection of it, neither of these can exist in the highest and purest level of Light, which is of the Spirit rather than of the material plane. And this truth that our outer form must ultimately dissolve itself into Light was known for centuries in the Mystery School tradition in which I was trained.

We are essentially Children of the Light, and although we borrow forms for a time, they are not our real nature, and in the end to return to that real nature, we must surrender all our forms, even the soul level form, so that we can once more become one with the Light. But when we return to the Light, we return with the seed-wisdom of everything that we have learned here, so that we return with a great harvest to enrich the Source from which we came.

Comment by Stuart: This last exchange shows the depth of understanding that sustained all of Mary Magdalene's teaching. Here her training in the Isis Temple in Alexandria comes into its own, and she shows her mastery of the Mystery School teaching on the symbolism of Light. Light was one of the central symbols used in most of the ancient Mystery Schools, and the relationship of Light with form is an interesting one.

There is a resonance here with our first book, *The Essenes: Children of the Light.* In the quotation that introduces Part Fourteen of that book, we quote from *The Emerald Tablets of Thoth the Atlantean,* translated by M. Doreal, and this speaks of the need to "become formless" before one can merge completely with the Light.

23. The Final Farewell

This book developed in a series of breakthroughs and connections with others who added their pieces to the emerging picture, but by April 2011, it looked as if all the work of writing had been completed. However, we were soon to discover that there was one more surprise in store for us. During that month of April, our friend Pete Stickland came to us for a past life session. In the middle of this process, the Energy changed, and Pete was able to speak from a level of deep insight.

After the session, Joseph of Arimathea came through and told us that Pete was speaking from his memory of the last Gnostic Gathering on Cyprus. Joseph continued: "These words were to be remembered by all of those present so we could bring them forward at some future time when we had agreed we would all come together again." Later on, Alariel and his group of angels checked the wording with the Akashic Records, making one or two small changes and adding Mary's final remarks at the end. And Alariel also gave me some more information to set this into perspective.

Alariel: By the time the final Gathering was held, it was clear that the lives of these Gnostics were getting progressively more difficult, and most of them realized that this would be the last opportunity for the whole group to meet together. At this intensely emotional time, Mary Magdalene spoke for all of them, and her words reflect the deep feelings within the group.

Now you are reaching the end of another cycle, and intense emotions are surfacing again within the Essene Soul Family. It is against this background of parallel times that the events of the recent Gathering in March of this year should be seen. It was not an accident that Pete came to experience a past life at this special time, and it was his ability to balance energies and his strong link with Mary Magdalene which has made this breakthrough possible.

Comment by Stuart: What follows is the information that came through in Pete's session and the extra material which Alariel provided at the end to complete Mary's statement. I believe this is one of the key statements by Mary, as it shows the depth of her understanding of the core Energy of Love.

Mary Magdalene: We are the ones who know the joy of Love, the joy of union. We are the ones who know the true connection with one another—we are not separate. We recognize this connection as Love. No words are needed here, and this Love includes everything. Within this Love nothing is hidden, and there is nothing to hide.

Here there are no boundaries, for we know that Love is infinite. There is nothing that is not included within this Love, and nothing extra is needed. Here we are aware of one another as pure Light, pure Love, pure Consciousness. It is so easy to be Love, to hold this Energy, and I wonder why we would choose any other existence. We ask that others may know of this Reality so that they, too, may choose Love.

And now we know that we must move into other realms that are not so full of Love, yet if all is well, these, too, may be raised up into the Light. There is so much beauty in the physical realm—Mother Earth is so beautiful. There is so much life here, and we are so deeply connected to Mother Earth as she is connected to Father Sun, our shining Star. At a deep level of experience, all is One, and the sign of this Oneness is the great gift of Love that connects us all.

It is so good to know that I have a spiritual Family that walks with me, a Family that knows the Truth—with this Family I can be who I really am. It is so good to remember this time together, and when we go out into the world, we will carry the Energy of Love with us. When we all meet again, perhaps in other lives wearing other faces, we will recognize this golden Energy and know that we have connected again with the great Family of Love.

So go out now into the world with courage and with joy, taking the Energy of Love with you, and let this Energy spread out like golden ripples until the whole world is blessed and unified.

May Love fill your hearts always,
and may the angels bless you
and guide you upon your path.

Part Three:

The Sacred Earth

Native American wisdom
is deeply rooted
in the Sacred Universe
and the Sacred Earth.

Alariel

24. The Web of Life

Comment by Stuart: To place the theme of the Sacred Universe within a modern context, I have devoted Part Three of this book to the celebrated speech by Chief Seattle. He was the leader of the Suquamish and Duwamish tribes of the east central Puget Sound area on the American Pacific northwest coast. He made his speech in December 1854 as part of treaty negotiations with the U.S. government.

There are two main versions of the speech, one recorded by witness Dr. Henry Smith and a more realistic text developed in 1969 by Professor William Arrowsmith of the University of Texas. Arrowsmith read this version of the Speech in 1970 at an Earth Day rally attended by his colleague, Professor Ted Perry.   With Arrowsmith's permission, Perry used the text as the basis for a film script which was inspired by Chief Seattle's words.

I am most grateful to Ted Perry for permission to quote from this script in producing my own version of the speech, which I give here. This version is based on channeling the consciousness of Chief Seattle and projecting the speech he would give today to an enlightened and environmentally aware audience.   (See also the Further Reading section under Gifford.)

The Web of Life

Every part of the Earth
is sacred to my people.
Every hillside and every valley
has been touched by some happy memory
or sad event in the life of my people.
Every island, every stream,
every path among the tall trees
has shared our moments of joy
or consoled us in times of sorrow.
Every river, every mountain, every lake
has shared our aspirations and our dreams.
Every shining pine needle,
every sandy shore,
every mist in the dark woods,
every meadow and humming insect
is holy in the memory and experience of my people.

The sap which courses through the trees
carries the memories of the red man.
Even the stones along the seashore
resonate with the memories of my people.
The ground beneath our feet responds
more lovingly to our steps than to yours,
for it holds the ashes of our grandfathers.
The Earth is rich with the echoes of our kin,
and our bare feet know the kindred touch.

We are part of the Earth
and she is part of us.
The perfumed flowers are our sisters,
and the deer, the horse, the great eagle
are our brothers.
The rocky crests,

the juices in the meadows,
the body heat of the pony,
all these belong to the same family—
a sacred family, for it comes from a sacred Source,
the Creator of all things.
Man also is a member of this family,
the sacred family of life.

And when we kill a living thing
so that our children may have food,
we ask permission to do this
and respect the sacrifice the animal has made.
To us, all life is sacred,
and being sacred, it demands respect.

And so if we decide to sell our land,
remember it is sacred.
Teach your children it is sacred
so that they may know
that each reflection in the quiet water of the lakes
tells of events within the story of my people.
Thus the loud voice of the thunder
echoes the sound of war-drums.
Soft falling snow
whispers of a time
of clarity and healing,
and the rainbow reminds us
of a time of joy.

In the rustling of the moonlit leaves
I hear the singing of my grandmother,
and the river's murmur
echoes with the voices of my kin.
The air is precious to the red man,
for all things share the same breath:
the animal, the tree, the man.

The air that gave my grandfather his first breath
also receives his final sigh.

So if we sell you this land,
remember to keep some wild and untamed places
where you can taste the wind
sweetened by the perfume of meadow flowers.
And leave some little corner of your lives
also untamed and free
beyond the clockwork tyranny of time.
In that free space enjoy,
as we have done,
the waves lapping gently on the shore
and the crystal sparkle of a mountain stream,
the swiftness of the horse
and the soaring of the eagle,
the beauty of a sunset
and the cool clarity of dawn,
the feeling of sand beneath your feet
as you walk along a beach
and the magic of snow painting the hills
with a carpet of white,
the shimmering of fine rain upon a cobweb
and a seabird calling somewhere in the mist,
the rustling of leaves in a dark wood
and the evening talk of frogs around a pond,
the wonder of stars on a clear night
and the silver mystery of the moon.

And when you journey out into the land,
out into this country that once was ours,
stop for a moment when you hear
some bird sing sweetly on the morning air
or see the fragile beauty of a butterfly,
or come to some place where the view
touches a chord within your heart.

And know that when you do,
it has touched our hearts also
and made a long journey seem shorter
with a moment of joy.
And give thanks to the Creator who has made
all the wonder and beauty of this sacred Earth.
And all these things,
so precious to us,
may become precious to you also.
And if your children
and your children's children
receive from this land
only a tenth of all the joy and blessings
that my people have received,
then they will count themselves as rich indeed.

We have been the guardians of this land,
this place which the Creator gave to us,
and to sell this land is no small thing.
This is no desert place
for it teems with many living things.
So if we sell you all this land,
love it and care for it as we have done.
And if we sell this land,
you must treat the creatures of this place
as your brothers,
for all things share in the web of life.
What is man without the creatures of the Earth?
If all the animals were gone,
man would die from a great loneliness of spirit.
Whatever happens to the creatures of the Earth
soon happens to man,
for all things are connected.

The Earth is our Mother.
This we know.

The Earth does not belong to man,
man belongs to the Earth.
This we know.
All things are connected
like the blood which unites one family.
All things are connected,
and whatever happens to the Earth,
happens to the sons of the Earth.
Man did not weave the web of life,
he is merely a strand in it.
Whatever he does to the web,
he does to himself.

The power of the Creator
flows through this web of life,
and the Creator put us here
as the guardians of this land.
As guardians we recognize
that all livings things have their own way
and their own purpose.
This should be respected.

The Earth, our Mother,
nourishes us
and provides a place
where we may tread our path.
And all the joys and sorrows of our life
are lessons bringing us
little by little,
to balance and the Greater Harmony.
This Harmony embraces all,
the living and the dead,
and every plant and creature,
stone and star throughout the universe.

All aspects of Creation
share in this Great Harmony,
and every form of life
contains an Essence planted deep within
by the Creator's power.
This sacred Essence is the source of our respect
for every living thing,
and this is what we honor
in the rocks and trees.

We see ourselves,
not as a separate or a sovereign force
but as a strand within the web of life,
a strand dependent on the other strands
as they depend on us.
Living in Harmony with all of life,
we watch the cycles of the sun and moon,
the lesser cycles and the greater ones,
within the flowing pattern of the Whole.
This understanding gives our lives
a place within the scheme of things,
a deeper meaning,
and a purpose that transcends
the sharpest sorrows and the sweetest joys.

The knowledge of this Harmony
illumines all our living like a star
and lies behind our wish
to live in peace with you.
This Harmony is woven deep within our people,
and it forms the wellspring of our dreams,
our greatest aspirations,
and the inmost longings of our hearts.
It runs so deep within us
that we do not often
speak about these things.

I speak of them today
so you will understand
why we should now consider
selling all this land that is so precious
and so much a part of us.
And if we do agree to this,
I hope we may live out
the twilight of our race,
our few remaining days,
in peace.

Yet when the last red man
has vanished from the Earth,
and his memory is just another legend,
like a cloud drifting across the winter sky,
these shores and forests will still hold
the spirits of my people.
The proud warriors and profound old men,
the kind mothers and wise grandmothers,
the children who played amongst the sunlit trees
and were so happy here—
all these still love the lonely places of this land.

And when your children's children
venture out and think they are alone
in the fields and on the plains,
upon the hills, or in the quiet woods,
they will not be alone.
For every corner of this land
is thronged with the returning spirits of my people,
gentle spirits who once roamed
these hills and valleys,
shores and lakes
throughout the golden summer of our race.

So be just
and deal kindly with my people.
For the dead are everywhere among you,
and they hold the power to haunt
the deep recesses of your inmost dreams.

Part Four:

Mary Magdalene in Perspective

> Mary understood the Kingdom of Heaven better than any of the other disciples.
>
> Daniel Benezra

25. A Woman of Mystery

When we first started researching Mary Magdalene, in comparison with many of the other New Testament figures, she seemed both remote and mysterious. There were references to her in the Gnostic Gospels, but as these are constrained by a question and answer format, Mary was never able to speak at any length. The result is like a incomplete mosaic with many tiny pieces but not enough to assemble a coherent picture. Even her own gospel, *The Gospel of Mary*, is fragmentary. Only eight of the eighteen pages have survived, and this means that 56% of the text is missing. The result of this situation is clear: we have never heard the real voice of Mary Magdalene, which is why she remains so much a mystery.

As our researches continued, and Alariel agreed to talk at length about Mary Magdalene's identity, she began to come into a clearer focus for us. When we learned that after the death of her father, she had entered Joseph of Arimathea's house in Jerusalem at the age of eight *as his adopted daughter,* this single revelation changed our whole perception of Mary. Suddenly she ceased to be an outsider, a stranger, and instead became one of the inner circle surrounding the young Jeshua.

When Alariel describes their "one magical year together" as children before they each went upon their own journey of spiritual exploration and self-realization, the foundations are already being put in place for their later meeting as adults. And when he adds that even as children they "became aware of a powerful spiritual bond that extended over many lifetimes," he is beginning to reveal the real and enduring nature of their relationship—and the secret of why they were able to work together in such perfect harmony. This is beginning to sound, not like some chance meeting of unconnected souls, but more like the working out of some Grand Strategy—and perhaps even an account of a great love story extending over many lives.

When we began this series of books, our knowledge of Mary Magdalene was very limited indeed. Looking back now, we can see that we lacked even the most basic information about her—for example, we did not know her full name. "Mary Magdalene" is a way of identifying her as "Mary of Bethany" or "James, son of Zebedee" identifies these individuals, but it is not her full name. Although attempts have been made to link Mary with Magdala near Galilee, the truth is that "Magdalene" is a distinction rather than a reference to the name of a place. Deriving from the Hebrew word *migdal* meaning "a tower," it identifies a person who, for a time at least, withdraws from the world to pursue a spiritual path. It also carries a *sense of isolation* in the quest for Truth in contrast to *integration* into the life of the world as a householder.

So when Alariel talked about her identity, we learned that her name was Myriam, but information on her second name came to us from a different source. When Lyn relived her past life experience in Israel, Mary Magdalene was first of all identified by the name "Anne" with the extended form of the name—"Mary Anne" emerging later in the session. This was a vital piece of information because now putting all this together, we knew her full name: Myriam Anne of Tyana.

But when we started looking at traditional sources of information on Mary, they proved much more restricted. The Biblical account gives only tantalizingly brief references to her, and even when we were working on our first book, *The Essenes: Children of the Light,* we had no real idea of her true significance. In Chapter 16 of that book, we describe the existence of a highly secret group within the Essene Brotherhood called "the Core Group." When Daniel first described this organization, he told us, "Only a few elders in each community know of it. You could live and work in an Essene community for the whole of your life and never hear anyone talk about the core group." Gradually we pieced together information on this, the most secret of all aspects of the Essenes, and a picture emerged of an inner group which supported the work of Jeshua and was responsible to some extent for his safety. And one of the surprises when we got a list of all the seven core group members was that Mary Magdalene was there in this inner and most secret Essene group.

At the time, that information did intrigue us, and we wondered, *Why was Mary Magdalene sitting in a group operating at the highest level of the Essene Brotherhood—a group that also included Joseph of Arimathea, his sister Mother Mary, her husband Joseph, their son James and Mary's nephew John? What was this mysterious Mary*

Magdalene doing in such august company?

As the information for that first book continued to roll in, our perception of Mary Magdalene changed radically. However, even at that stage we became aware that there were undercurrents in Jewish society moving against her. Here, for example, is Daniel attempting to describe briefly Mary Magdalene.

Daniel: Mary was a person of great virtue and authority, gained through many lives. She was like a priestess, a person of great intensity. We Essenes recognized her power and her lineage. We recognized what she had achieved. Not everyone did so. Some were very ready to dismiss her, especially when they heard of her connections with Egypt.

Clearly it was her training in the Isis Temple at Alexandria which both alarmed and frightened the more conventional disciples and turned them against her. Bear in mind that all the more conventional Jews like the Pharisees would have regarded the Isis wisdom tradition as a *pagan and heathen cult*—a view not shared by the progressive Essenes, who were very happy to send their daughters for training in the Mystery School there. However, that conventional view was very common in the wider Jewish society of that time. A Priestess in the Isis tradition would have been regarded with fear and loathing by both the Pharisees and the Sadducees at that period. When one becomes aware of this, the opposition to Mary amongst the wider group of disciples, including Andrew and his brother Peter, becomes much easier to understand. They were just reflecting the common prejudices in their society and were not expressing a particularly extreme view.

Although this undercurrent of resistance to and suspicion of Mary Magdalene remained as a recurring theme in our researches, we also noticed a counterbalancing theme of elevating Mary into the very close circle around Jeshua. (In our first book we used the traditional name "Jesus," and we only came to realize that he was never called by this name as our researches for the second book unfolded.) Here, for example, is Daniel in Chapter 26 of *The Essenes: Children of the Light:*

Daniel: Although Jesus was far beyond any of us, yet I saw that Mary Magdalene was more his equal than we were. Of course, both the masculine and feminine energies are aspects of the greater Divine energies and as Essenes, we knew the symbolism of the Father and the Mother very well. Yet I could sense that there was some even deeper mystery in their relationship, a mystery that went beyond my understanding. When they were together within one of the inner groups, there were moments when great energies seemed to focus through them, giving even the simplest movement a special power and grace.

Comment by Stuart: As our research continued, our understanding of the real significance of Mary Magdalene deepened and clarified. And when Alariel revealed to us the twofold pattern of special development which Jeshua had planned—an outer

Church and an inner Mystery School—all this became much clearer. Here is Alariel explaining this pattern of development in Chapter 11 of *Power of the Magdalene.*

Alariel: Above all, Peter could not accept the basic structure through which the Way would be spread—that after Jeshua left them, the teachings would be given out in two ways. The outer teachings would be spread by most of the male disciples, led by Peter, who was to be *the rock*, the foundation of this new movement. Whilst the inner teachings (the Inner Mysteries of the Way) would be taught by John, James, Thomas, and Philip, this group being led by Mary Magdalene.

Comment by Stuart: Peter's failure to accept Mary's leading role as the Keeper of the Inner Mysteries and the leader of the Mystery School of the Way had far-reaching effects. By distancing himself from Mary Magdalene, Peter made the persecution of the Gnostics possible and by refusing to accept a leadership role for a woman within the new Christian movement, he began the long road that led to the disempowerment of women within the Church—an issue that continues to blight the spiritual life of the West to the present day.

Yet despite all the controversy that continues to surround her, one can discern a powerful trend that has resulted in Mary Magdalene being honored, loved, and revered throughout the world. And at the heart of this positive perception of Mary Magdalene lies the undeniable greatness of her achievement.

By merging with the All, Mary Magdalene was able to transcend time and enter such a fundamental level of Truth that even today her words seem fresh, modern, and full of wisdom and inspiration. If you compare the Magdalene Summaries with any of the Gnostic Gospels, you will see what a remarkable distance Mary had traveled. By striking out courageously into such a fundamental level of Truth, she has become a beacon to illuminate even the dark places of our own time.

In a very real sense, Mary Magdalene is the first modern woman. Enlightened, empowered, courageous and compassionate, she demonstrates a respect for all life. In doing so, she has become a Heroine of the Western World—a heroine who is now ready to come into her own, sweep aside all the distortions and the lies, and stand forth as one of the ultimate icons for our time.

26. A Spiritual Partnership

Alariel: The key to understanding the whole life-pattern of Mary Magdalene is her spiritual partnership with Jeshua. All the long years of preparation and training only make sense within the greater context of this partnership.

The nature of their preparation was quite different and yet complementary. Jeshua's preparation was outward and dynamic in its focus, traveling across much the ancient world and connecting with many traditions and ways of communicating the truth. Mary's preparation was very different in being inward-focused and receptive in its nature, cloistered within the walls of a temple in which the innermost secrets of the Isis tradition were revealed to her. When Joseph of Arimathea went to Tyana, he went to adopt Mary-who-was-not-yet-Magdalene. Through her intense inner training in the Isis Temple, Mary *became* the Magdalene—the strong Tower of Wisdom rooted in the earth and yet pointing to the heavens, a vital connection between humanity and the All.

There is one day—and one event—that marks the transition from the long years of preparation to the beginning of their real work in the world, and that is the day that Jeshua returns to Jerusalem. He had left as a boy of twelve and returns as a man of thirty. Mary had left as a girl of nine, and she comes back from Alexandria two weeks before Jeshua's return, going straight to Joseph's house in Jerusalem. Using her now complete powers as a High Priestess of Isis, Mary attunes to Jeshua's consciousness and is able to merge with him and see through his eyes. That is how she knows exactly where he is on the road between Jerusalem and the coast, where he has disembarked from one of Joseph's ships.

Taking a small pitcher with her, Mary goes out to meet Jeshua, and chooses a village to the west of Jerusalem where there is a well by the roadside. The meeting at the well is a real one, but it is also deeply symbolic: this will be a meeting of two Initiates who have drunk deeply from the well of Ageless Wisdom.

Jeshua arrives, hot and dusty in the midday sun, and there is Mary with the pitcher from which he drinks. That simple act is symbolic of Mary offering him all the knowledge, all the wisdom, she has acquired in her years of training in the Isis tradition. And having drunk, Jeshua likens the pitcher to their long years of preparation,. and he breaks it upon the stonework of the well to show that all this is now over, and they are entering a new phase in their lives.

And Jeshua takes Mary's hand and says, 'Mary, this day our real work begins. Let us go hand in hand into Jerusalem, as a sign that we are beginning our Ministry together.'

Comment by Stuart: Although that Ministry is well-documented, the teachings which Mary gave as her Summaries on the island of Cyprus were lost for many centuries. Here is Alariel's reflection on the importance of those Magdalene Summaries.

Alariel: The Summaries give a concise but comprehensive survey of Mary's teachings on key areas of knowledge. Taken together, these Summaries form a complete outline of Mary Magdalene's philosophy, a philosophy enriched by her life as a leading Essene, her training in the Isis Temple at Alexandria, and her life as the spiritual partner of Jeshua. She learned a great deal from Jeshua, but as someone trained as a High Priestess in the Isis tradition, she had her own store of wisdom, and it must be said that Jeshua also learned a great deal from her!

Of course some of what Mary said will be challenging—but it was challenging all those centuries ago on the island of Cyprus. Consider for a moment what Mary was doing: she was teaching a series of Master-classes on the nature of Reality!

Comment by Stuart: Now more than at any other time in history, we need this information because we need to know what the Real is and what the source of our illusions is. At a time of Transition, human beings need to let go of the story, the drama, the illusion, and step into the Real. If Mary can help us to do this, she will have given us a gift beyond price.

The session with Alariel continues.

Alariel: Now 2,000 years have passed and your planet has reached the end of a planetary cycle, and at this point there is a gathering and concentrating of the energies of time. When a planet goes into Transition, the most intense spiritual energies generated on that planet *at any time in its history* return and come into focus again to reprise that achievement. You may think of it as a celebration of the past peaks of human achievement, but this also has a practical purpose: it assists humanity in accessing the highest spiritual levels of which it is capable, levels which are invaluable when entering a global process of transformation and ascension.

In the case of planet Earth, the energies of Jeshua and Mary Magdalene are now returning in all their original intensity, which is why it is so much easier for the souls who experienced these energies 2,000 years ago to access them again.

That is why the teachings of Mary Magdalene are now being returned to you: the teachings of Jeshua may have been misinterpreted, but they were never lost. Yet the Earth has not heard the real voice of Mary Magdalene for 2,000 years, and it is time for that voice and the wisdom it carries to go out into the world.

27. The Philosophy of
Mary Magdalene

It is only in her later teaching in Languedoc, Avalon (see Chapter 16 of *Power of the Magdalene*) and on Cyprus that Mary Magdalene really comes into her own as a spiritual teacher. When she does so, she reveals herself as not merely a brilliant and intelligent pupil of Jeshua but a powerful and original thinker in her own right: one of the great philosophers of her time.

It may seem strange to use the word "philosopher" in connection with Mary Magdalene, but this is the only word that can accurately describe her achievement in laying the intellectual foundations of the Gnostic movement. If one accepts this assessment of Mary Magdalene, the full injustice of her treatment at the hands of the early Church Fathers becomes clear.

Here are Alariel's comments on that situation.

Alariel: The truth is that the early Church Fathers were quite unable to stomach the idea of Mary Magdalene as a philosopher and a leader in the intellectual life of the Western world. So they trashed her words in the Gnostic Gospels and went on to destroy her reputation as a woman. And some time later, the leaders of this same Church destroyed the only culture built upon Mary's ideas—the Cathars.

It has been the role of the vandal throughout history to trash everything that he cannot understand. However, these ecclesiastical vandals were not to know that in the present century, the Church they loved would be in a state of turmoil while the star of Mary Magdalene would shine ever brighter in the Western consciousness. They had fought a long bitter and dirty campaign against Mary Magdalene, and yet here she is now rising serenely above them—serenely because she had fought *not at all*—she had simply seen and known and taught and loved— and in her understanding of the All, she has triumphed.

Her triumph vindicates the Mystery School tradition of the West and the Sisterhood of Isis in which she shines as a bright star. That tradition includes the teachings of the great Sage who was known both as Hermes and as Thoth, who brought non-duality to the West under the name of the Principle of Polarity. When you read the Magdalene Summaries that Mary gave on the island of Cyprus, you see how much she kept the faith of that Hermetic tradition, and you begin to see Mary Magdalene for the first time as the most wonderful and courageous teacher— someone who was not afraid to speak

Truth at whatever the cost. But you also see her great heart, her deep compassion for all forms of life, and the love that included everyone that she encountered.

Mary's thorough training as a High Priestess of Isis gave her a sense of detachment from her early upbringing within the Essene tradition. Once she had reached the very peak of achievement within the Isis system, she was able to speak, not from a traditional context, but from a direct knowledge of ageless wisdom. That knowledge enabled Mary to cut through the complex jungle of Gnostic theology and present a very different perspective that offered a clear and practical path to the Light.

It was the genius of Mary Magdalene to put things simply, directly, and yet profoundly.

The secret wisdom of Mary Magdalene—a deep level of wisdom that she could share at that time only with the most advanced seekers of the Truth—is universal in its nature. It brings together the wisdom of East and West into a synthesis that represents the whole of the Earth and not just part of it. Mary was able to transcend the traditions which had nurtured her and soar up into a universal understanding of the All.

This understanding not only spans space in uniting the enlightened beings of all galaxies but also spans time so that all

enlightened ones share in the same deep
knowledge and experience of Oneness.

As a Master of Oneness,
Mary Magdalene stands
as a jewel of human achievement,
a great soul and a great philosopher.
It is time for all the world
to acknowledge that greatness.

Comment by Stuart: In our first book, *The Essenes:
Children of the Light,* I relived my life as the Essene
elder, Daniel Benezra.   Here is Daniel's final
assessment of Mary Magdalene.

Daniel: Mary was one of the most *awake* people
that I ever met. She brought this sense of
focused alertness and present awareness
to everything she did. Compared to her,
most of the people I encountered were
sleepwalking through their lives.

28. Summation: The Lady Magdalene

Two thousand years ago I saw
my Teacher stand supreme,
and I saw him walking hand in hand
with the Lady Magdalene.

Two thousand years have passed since then
and faded like a dream.
The time has come to honor her,
the Lady Magdalene.

The lies can never dim her star
or make her less serene.
She is the brightest and the best—
the Lady Magdalene.

Part Five: East and West

When there is no duality,
all things are one
and nothing can be separate.
The enlightened ones
of all times and places
have entered into this truth.

On Faith in the Heart by Sosan

29. The Coming Together of East and West

Alariel: The teachings of Mary Magdalene were the culmination of the whole arc of Essene and Gnostic development: she was able to extend the original Essene impulse into the full flowering of Gnostic ideas.

Mary Magdalene and the apostle John were the only two original thinkers to emerge from the group around Jeshua, and the power of Mary's understanding of the All inspired many who heard her speak.

Mary has been seen for so long as a minor character in the drama centered upon Jeshua that it has been difficult to assess the scale of her achievement. But now the time has come to measure that achievement on a world stage and weigh up what she accomplished.

Mary Magdalene's profound understanding of the nature of Reality places her on an equal footing with Sosan, the author of the classic Zen text *On Faith in the Heart.*

Many other philosophers, especially in Buddhism, Hinduism, and Taoism, have expressed non-duality at some length, but only these two great thinkers managed to produce a concise overview of non-duality and the nature of the Real. They link West and East in a unique achievement and should be honored equally. Significantly, their contributions are marked by a directness and brevity which make them uniquely accessible to the modern mind.

Think of a great pyramid: at the base all traditions seem to be very far apart. Yet as you climb up the pyramid towards enlightenment at the topmost point, perceptions change—and all the traditions begin to come together. This is what is happening now. As you move through the combination of personal and planetary Transition, East and West will increasingly come together in greater levels of respect and understanding. That is why it is appropriate at this point to shift the focus of this book and honor a great spiritual pioneer from the East.

> Now that you have seen
> the full extent of Mary's teachings,
> you are well-prepared
> for what is to follow.
> Open your mind to it
> and look for many parallels
> with the wisdom of Mary Magdalene.

30. The Way of Oneness

Note by Stuart: The author of this classic Zen text was Kanchi Sosan, the original Chinese form of his name being variously given as Chien-chih Seng ts'an or Jianzhi Sengcan. He was the third Zen Patriarch: the year and place of his birth are uncertain, but it is known that he died in the year 606 CE. Little is known about Sosan, but it seems that he lived the whole of his life in China.

The title of this poem, the *Xin Xin* (or *Hsin Hsin) Ming,* has no universally agreed translation. An article by Professor Pajin lists eighteen options with a number of permutations of Faith/Belief and Heart/Mind. In this chapter I have given a shortened version of the text, covering about one third of the original. In preparing this new version, I have tried to present these ideas in a way which has real resonance for the modern Western reader. I have also put spaces between the sections to break up the text and make it more readable.

There is nothing difficult
about the Way of Oneness
when picking and choosing are set aside
and all is accepted.
Once you stop longing and loathing,
everything becomes clear

but make even the smallest preference,
and your whole world is divided.

If you wish to see the Truth,
live with an open mind
and do not be for or against anything.
To swing between extremes of liking and disliking
is a sickness of the mind . . .

Do not get entangled in the outer world
or lost in the inner emptiness,
stay serene in the Oneness of things
and duality vanishes by itself . . .

Talking and thinking
turn you from the harmony of the Way:
stop talking and thinking,
and you may experience Reality . . .

The changes that seem to happen
in the outer world of form
are like the shadows of a dream.
They seem real because of our ignorance.
Do not go searching for the truth—
just throw away your opinions!

Avoid all aspects of duality—
it's illusion trying to deceive you again!
All dualities come from the One,
but do not cling to the One either!
If you do, there will be the One
and you-clinging-to-the-One.

When the heart is at peace with the Way,
nothing in the world offends—
no blame, no thing, no mind.

In the emptiness the mind is silent,
and the heart is unified and whole.
All the components of the Universe
have returned to their origins,
and the many are again One . . .

To cling is to lose one's balance:
open the hands, the mind, the heart,
and let it all go!
Let all be as it is:
flowing with the Way,
you wander along,
free to be yourself . . .

Cling to nothing and accept everything—
that is the path to the Light . . .

Awakened, there are no extremes
and no opposites—just a continuum of Oneness.
All the pairs of opposites are illusory dreams—
why try to grasp them?
Gain and loss, better and worse, greater and
lesser—throw them all out!

When awake, we see the Real,
not the dreams.
If the heart does not judge or choose,
then all things are as they are—
they are One . . .

When you see Reality
as a mystical whole,
the cool essence of being
pours into you,
and you return to your true nature.
Here there is nothing to remember

and nothing to do.
All is empty, clear, and full of Light.

In the realm of the Real,
there is neither self nor other:
awareness simply is.
To come into harmony with the Real,
just say, "Not Two."
When there is no duality,
all things are one and nothing can be separate:
the enlightened ones of all times and places
have entered into this truth . . .

One Life in all beings,
all beings within one Web
of Consciousness and Life.
If this is understood, you are home already,
and there is no need to worry about being perfect.

When duality vanishes,
you enter true freedom.
Here words fail,
for this is a state beyond language:
in the Real, there is no past, present, or future,
only the Eternal Now.

Note: Details of the eleven English translations of
the *Xin Xin Ming* are given at the end of the Further
Reading section, and the complete text of this new
version can be found in the Epilogue.

Part Six:

The Old and the New

It is a paradox that Mary Magdalene,
drawing upon two ancient traditions,
should have been able to develop
a presentation that now seems
fresh, new, and relevant to your time.

Alariel

31. The Emergence of Gnostic Zen

Alariel: There is clearly no historical link between the Gnostics (who did not survive beyond the third century of the Common Era) and the first pioneer of Zen, Bodhidharma, who lived in the early fifth century CE. However, linear time gives only one level of understanding, and there are deeper perspectives which tell a different story.

Many of the souls who encountered non-duality with advanced Gnostic groups in the early years of Christianity went on to explore that theme in greater depth during lives in Ch'an and Zen monasteries. Once a soul has a theme firmly in its sights, it can be tenacious in following up this theme in subsequent lives. That is why the Gnostic movement and Zen have such a deep connection—a connection made even more poignant by the fact that the Gnostics were not able to pursue the full arc of their natural development.

Now that you have been able to read Mary Magdalene's Summaries, you can see that the Gnostic movement was developing in a direction, which if it had been able to continue, would have established it as a Western counterpart to Zen. Although very different in history and methods, these two traditions were essentially working towards the same goal. Even their primary symbol—Light—is identical for Gnostics and Mahayana Buddhists. With this in mind, it is quite logical to name this area of common ground 'Gnostic Zen.'

For most of the last 2,000 years while your culture writhed in the grip of duality, the words of Sosan would have seemed quite meaningless in the West. It is only now, as you approach the planetary Transition that his words acquire a new significance. As your obsession with duality fades, your consciousness begins to open out to other ways of exploring what Mary Magdalene called 'The All.' This is why so many points of resonance can now be seen between these traditions. Scan through the Magdalene Summaries given by Mary on the island of Cyprus and compare these with Sosan's remarkably concise and comprehensive outline of the nature of Reality. I think you will find many parallels. But as Sosan himself said,

> The enlightened ones
> of all times and places
> have entered into this truth.

Comment by Stuart: Many writers have noted parallels between Buddhism and Christianity, starting with Max Muller, continuing with Thomas Merton and including the modern author Elaine Pagels.

The link between Gnosis and Buddhism is less well-researched, but one could certainly cite the remarkable essay 'Buddhism and Gnosis' in *Further Buddhist Studies* by Edward Conze.

There are also some parallels in the terms used in these traditions:

Gnostic Term	Zen Term
Process	Practice
The All, Reality	Reality, the Real
The Way	The Great Way
Non-duality	Non-duality
Enlightened consciousness	Enlightenment

These resonances provide a clear indication of the existence of Gnostic Zen—something that perhaps we might even call *gno-zen*. At the highest point of both Gnostic and Zen systems, the concepts begin to come together and merge into a single transcendent level of understanding.

32: The Real Voice of
Mary Magdalene

Comment by Stuart: When the main revision of the manuscript for this book had been completed, Alariel shut down his channeling through me with the words, "Mission accomplished." He returned only once: in November 2011 to add some final comments placing *The Magdalene Version* within a larger context.

This final communication was a response to a manuscript called *Mary Magdalene Beckons: Join the River of Love*, which was sent to us by its author, Mercedes Kirkel. It was clear to me from the beginning that this manuscript contained information on Mary Magdalene that ran parallel with our own researches, and the messages from Mary in this book open a detailed insight into the practical side of her teachings. I recognized the wise and loving energy in these messages at once. It was the same energy I had encountered when channeling Mary's words for *The Magdalene Version*. (See the Further Reading section under Kirkel, Mercedes.)

Alariel: Please do not imagine that *The Magdalene Version* will go out into the world alone and unsupported. Because it is time for the real voice of Mary Magdalene to be heard, a number of channels throughout the world are now being inspired by Mary's energy. That energy will bring through the whole transmission of her teachings, and these will help to heal the Western consciousness through restoring the balance and focusing the Sacred Feminine.

Strands of wisdom from both the Essene and Isis traditions were brought together into a unique synthesis through the genius of Mary Magdalene and her work in communicating the Way has profound significance for the modern world. It is a paradox that Mary Magdalene, drawing upon two ancient traditions, should have been able to develop a presentation that now seems fresh, new, and relevant to your time.

Jeshua and Mary both aimed for simplicity in their teaching, but they achieved this in different ways. Jeshua took the element of story in the Jewish tradition and gave it new life through parables. Mary used another method: powerful, direct, and simple speech, which essentially became the vehicle for energy focusing through the heart. Other teachers spoke from the head to the head. Mary spoke from heart to heart. Though remarkable and refreshing today, this came with all the force of a revolution to Mary's audience—an audience used to struggling with the dense symbolism and complex language of the ancient world.

When you listen to Mary's words—words that have been lost to Western consciousness for 2,000 years, you begin to realize her true greatness as a teacher and mentor. Here we see a great mind distilling all the complexities of her age down into simple and timeless statements of truth.

Part Seven:

Transition and Beyond

It is both a continuous arc of change
and an opportunity from your point of view.
There is now a swift route into the Light,
a route enabling you to go through change
in lighter and easier ways.

Alariel in chapter 24 of *Beyond Limitations:*
The Power of Conscious Co-Creation

33. Karma in a Time of Transition

As we move into the planetary Transition, there is a lot of confusion about what will happen to our karma. How will we be able to clear all our karma, and what will happen to unresolved karma? We asked Alariel to comment on that issue, and this was his response.

Alariel: You are in process of passing through your planetary Transition when the Earth will move upwards into a new frequency, and there is a parallel development within your experience as human beings. You are leaving behind the heavy third dimensional (or 3D) experience and entering the much lighter world of the fifth dimension (or 5D.) Much has been written about the karma which you have accumulated during all your previous lives on this planet, so the question arises, 'What will happen to all this karma?' The answer is twofold.

The resolving of karmic energies depends mainly upon the existence of linear 3D time. When a planet enters Transition and moves into the next dimensional reality, 3D time vanishes. However, preparations for this are made well before you reach this point. During the run-up to the period preceding the transition period, human beings have steadily become more sensitive and more introspective, and many new therapies have emerged to help you deal with unresolved past life energies.

Whereas previous generations were just focused on living during that life, for this generation, your past lives—and all the energies they bring with them—are beginning to loom large. This process is helped along by the proliferation of physical ailments. When some past life energy emerges as an illness, human beings become very focused on dealing with the problem!

Now you could argue that it would have been wiser to resolve past life problems as you progressed through the whole sequence of lives, but it is a sad fact that most human beings have not lived like that. They have simply got on with expressing themselves in an ego-dominated way and have hardly given a second thought to any previous life they may have had. Well, all that is changing now. Your past lives (and the energies they bring) are no longer whispering at you; they are beginning to shout! And this shouting process is encouraging you to deal with these energies in a much more conscious and effective way than before.

Yet however effective you are, there is usually quite a lot of karma to deal with, and it is quite likely that at Transition some of this karmic energy remains unresolved. This is where the second aspect comes into focus. At the point of Transition, providing you are going through a process of awakening and rising in vibration, your remaining karma is waived through the operation of Divine Grace.

If you think about it, you will see that this must be done if there is to be any kind of justice. The linear time you need to resolve karma is disappearing, so soon no one will have the time to work off these energies in the traditional way through experiences in lives led at the 3D level. There just isn't going to be extended linear time for ego-dominated three dimensional lives—lives that certainly accumulated a lot of karma but were also an effective platform for paying off that karma, too.

In the quite exceptional situation that arises when a planet goes through Transition, other arrangements must be made to ensure that those who are capable of going into the experience of a higher level of being are able to do so. It would simply be unfair to hold back those souls who are capable of change and transformation just because they had some unresolved karma, which is why the intervention of Grace is essential at this time. Of course, this is an exceptional situation: a planet only goes through Transition once, and you have the good fortune to be living at this momentous time.

There is also another consideration here. It has always been possible to deal with karma in two ways: pay it back by working it off in the traditional way or transmute it. The key to transmuting karma is to probe the original energy, understand the cause, learn the lesson, release the energy, and move on. This process of transmuting karma can be done at any point whether you are working within linear time or not.

And another question arises here, too: won't you be acquiring more karma as you live your new lives beyond the point of Transition? Yes, but only for a little while. It will take human beings some time to move from creating their reality at the personality level with the ego dominating their lives to the next level of reality creation, which is focused on the soul. When the soul creates a reality, it does so with the highest good of *all beings* in mind: this is karma-less creation, and that is what you are now moving towards. Yes, it will take a little time to get used to this, but after Transition this new process, which is called Co-creation, will become more and more the model for human experience.

The whole point of moving beyond karma is to move to living in much lighter, easier, and more joyful ways. And that will form the basis of the exploration of life beyond the Transition. So don't think of the Transition as an ending of all things. Yes, it ends a planetary cycle, but life continues, and this is only the beginning of living in a much more expanded and enlightened way.

Life beyond the Transition will give you the chance to cast off your littleness and reconnect fully with the great Beings of Light you really are. So go forward into these times of change with courage. After all, you have nothing to lose but your limitations!

Comment by Stuart: In our third book, *Beyond Limitations: The Power of Conscious Co-Creation,* Alariel explores the three main levels on which we create our reality: Personal Reality Creation, Co-Creation (the level of the soul) and Instantaneous Creation (creating at the level of the Spirit.) Only the first level, creating at the level of the personality, is governed by the Law of Karma.

34. Truth and Transition

Alariel: Moving through your personal Transition will focus you as never before on the essential Truth: the half-truths and fudges that may have satisfied you in the past will now seem like sharp betrayals, and the search for the Truth and the Real will intensify in your life.

The Truth is actually very simple: *there is only one of us out there!* All the multitude of forms are like so many clothes that you may try on from the Great Wardrobe of the Universe, but to confuse any clothing—however splendid—with the inner essence of the One Spirit seems rather foolish. Yet such is the power of illusion that human beings confuse the outer form with the inner essence all the time.

This is what Transition really means: the journey out of illusion and into Reality, out of drama and into peace, out of story and into the All. Of course, you can stay in illusion if you wish, but that means that you will continue to be a spiritual child. Human beings have lived for many centuries as spiritual children, and they have dreamed and slumbered through huge expanses of limiting and disempowering time.

But now the Earth is sending humanity a wake-up call. It's time to let go of the illusion and see things as they really are. Then you will begin to function as a spiritual adult and be able to take your power back, for in truth your power was never stolen from you—instead, you gave it away. Giving away your power was part of the package of being a spiritual child. The responsibility of making decisions for yourself seemed too heavy a burden, so you let a family, a church, a regiment, a company, a trade union, or a state do that for you.

But now it is time for the veil of forgetfulness to start dissolving, so that you can see who you really are—a spiritual adult who is also a meta-gifted and multidimensional Being of Light. When you can glimpse that, even for a short while, you can begin to stand tall in the Light of your own consciousness. And compared to *that,* continuing to be a spiritual child doesn't seem such a good choice any more, and so you're ready to let it go and move on.

> What you are moving on into
> is nothing less than ascended Truth,
> unbroken consciousness,
> and Eternal Joy.
> All these are the rewards
> of an Awakening Humanity.
> All these are your birthright

and your destiny.
And the way to these goals
is *within you*
as it has always been.
You have never been more
than a heartbeat away
from Joy and Light
and all the Love
in the Universe!

You have searched the world to find the Light, and now you discover it was there all the time, deep inside of you like a seed waiting for the right time to burst into flower.

This is the time, this is the place, this is the moment to wake up and realize that the Light outside you and the Light inside you are One!

This is the time to focus on the Truth that can set you free: the truth about your own real nature as a Child of the Light and the truth about the universe—about the Reality in which you live and move. And when you realize that your own inner Self and the universe are not two things *but one thing*, everything in your life will change.

This is your moment of Transition,
your time of destiny.
Take courage
and let the Spirit within guide you
through the process
of transformation
that will lift you in vibration
and change your life *forever!*

35. The Totality of Being

Alariel: As you transform your being and your consciousness, you will increasingly be living across the total spectrum of human experience. Instead of concentrating upon one level—as you have done by focusing intensively on mental activity during the last few centuries—you will value all the four main levels and live in a balanced way that honors all of these. By balancing the Physical, Emotional, Mental and Spiritual levels—which we have called the PEMS Continuum—you can enjoy the full range of human experience and avoid the discomfort, disharmony, and dis-ease that comes from any kind of imbalance.

In one way it can be said that, apart from a brief period in Golden Atlantis, you have not really experienced what it is like to be fully, joyfully and radiantly human. Yes, you have lived in many human bodies, but they have staggered on from day to day, over-worked, under-nourished and ill with a whole host of addictions, karmic limitations and diseases. You may have accepted this as the norm for humanity, but to us it is a travesty of what human life should be and could be.

Comment by Stuart: We explore Golden Atlantis in our book, *Atlantis and the New Consciousness.*

The session with Alariel continues.

Alariel: To us, the ideal of human life is one where fear and want do not exist, and every day you rise up singing for the sheer joy of being alive. In our ideal, the human race enjoys a permanent state of peace, never goes to war and has no security industry of any kind. No one indulges in criminal activity because everyone enjoys high self-esteem and feels valued and loved. The individual lives in harmony with his or her society, and the whole of humanity resonates with the ideals of Light and Love. That state of being flows out into a changed relationship with the animal kingdom, which no longer reflects human fear, violence, and anger: a gentle vegetarian humanity now lives in peace with a gentle, vegetarian animal kingdom.

The link between human consciousness and the consciousness of the Earth now works to benefit both because humanity no longer pollutes and despoils the Earth Mother but respects and honors her. There are no violent events of weather, no volcanic activity, no floods, and no tidal waves. A peaceful and loving humanity lives in harmony with a peaceful and loving Earth.

Sounds very different from the experience of the average person nowadays, doesn't it? We are not saying that this ideal will be achieved five minutes after the Earth moves through Transition— this is the long term ideal for humanity, but it is an achievable ideal. So why have you failed to come anywhere near this ideal in the past?

Well, during the last 2,000 years, you settled for a lopsided development that denies the spiritual value of the physical level. The Essenes were far wiser than this: they balanced physical work in the fields and gardens in the morning with afternoon study and contemplation. And they honored the Earthly Mother just as much as the Heavenly Father.

But that, of course, goes to the heart of the problem: the Earthly Mother seemed far too close to pagan ideas for the early Church Fathers. In their desperation to avoid any sense of pagan contamination of their faith, the Church leaders split the human experience into the mental and spiritual (seen as potentially good) and the physical (seen as potentially bad). This had the effect of distorting the whole way in which you live, and that distortion has thrown up a series of problems within Western culture.

The last 2,000 years have provided an object-lesson in what happens when human beings ignore the Totality of Being and try to live in an artificial, restricted, and unnatural way, a way that ignores the human need to function in a state of balance. Human history abounds with examples that underline the central point: balance promotes all-round growth and development whereas imbalance always leads to some kind of problem down the line. Balance also means avoiding the kind of grim, life-denying seriousness that has characterized many Christian groups. They may have been serious about the pursuit of their faith, but all too often they lost sight of joy.

You may have got this balance wrong on a number of occasions in your past, but very soon as post-Transition humans, you will have a unique chance to get it right. You will be able to put your battle-scarred past behind you and make a new beginning. Part of the process of Awakening is to look at everything in a different way. Thus you will no longer perceive time as rigid and linear or karma as fixed and immutable, and above all you will start to see every experience as an opportunity to learn and grow.

By working with the soul through channeling, oracle systems, and past life processes, you can expand your ability to respond to subtle, intuitive, and multidimensional signals, and these signals will steadily push back the boundaries and limitations that have been restricting your consciousness. This process is joyful, empowering—even at times exhilarating—and the more you reach out to expand your awareness, the easier and more natural this will seem.

When your consciousness expands, your belief-system evolves to keep pace. Whilst in the past you thought in terms of rigid divisions and fixed structures, now everything begins to flow together in a continuum of being. Take the concept of past life work, for example. As you pass through the Transition where your planet moves out of linear time and into a new form of time which we might call Unified Time, you begin to focus much more on the Eternal Now and much less on the idea of past, present, and future. And gradually you will come to see your lives not as past lives at all but simply as lives— frequencies of energy and being that may be rooted in linear time but still flow out to modify and enrich other experiences. And the whole point of having these experiences is to learn from them and move your consciousness forward into new possibilities.

The process of opening and expanding your consciousness enables you to see the extent of the gift which these lives bring you. Every life is a potential opportunity to understand the vastness, the variety, the quality of your consciousness. Every life you have ever experienced is part of your own individual and unique tapestry, the pattern of expression that you—and you alone—could have chosen. Sometimes the pattern is enormously complex with many diversions and dead-ends or many forays into the darker side of human experience.

Yet however many times you explore darkness, the inner impulse to the Light— to joy, to love and to the aspirations of the soul—will bring you back on track within your chosen arc of spiritual development. You have woven this tapestry of lives in a highly unconscious way for many eons, but now at last you are reaching out towards the one ideal that makes sense— to become the multidimensional Beings that you really are.

When you go through THAT experience and emerge as fully-ascended Beings standing in the Light of your own consciousness, you will understand that every step upon the way, every limitation and every suffering was an essential component in the journey towards the expanding consciousness that you will then enjoy.

And when you stand victorious
on the peak of Ascension,
you will see that there is no waste,
there is no loss,
and every step of your journey
was a necessary step upon the road
to victory.

Part Eight:

The Essene Soul Family

When the last Essene community
disappears from the Earth,
our direct contact
with future generations
will vanish with it.
That is why we value these dialogues
and why so much information
has been given.

Daniel Benezra
in *The Essenes: Children
of the Light*

36. A Doorway to the Infinite

Comment by Stuart: When I began to follow the trail of past-life work with Joanna in the early 1990s, I thought I was just opening up a window on the past—a window that might provide some interesting information but would change nothing in my present life. How wrong I was!

Our past-life encounters led to contacts with people all over the world, and as that time in Israel came into focus for us—and we felt the love of our Teacher—what really opened up was a doorway to the Infinite.

By connecting with our expanded past-life selves, we started to glimpse the even greater Beings, which we and all the other Children of the Light really are! And by connecting with more and more people through our books, we have opened up possibilities that in those early days in the 1990s, we could never have dreamed of.

The series of books that I wrote with Joanna were never a solo effort but always a team process. As we wrote these books, our inner guidance—and the help we received from Alariel—gradually placed the narratives of our past-life subjects into a bigger context. This together with our contact with the Essene Brotherhood as a whole revealed a pattern of information that started simply and added fresh depth to the story with each new book. So in our first book, we describe Jeshua and Mary Magdalene as being spiritually very close, but only in producing our second book, did we learn that they were married as well as being spiritual partners. And with the books steadily gathering readers all over the world, the team grew bigger as new friends—who were really old friends returning—came to add their piece to the every-growing jigsaw.

Part of the process was the nature of these books as carriers of *energy* as well as containers for information. So many of our readers report that in the process of reading our books, the past—especially that past in Israel and the Isis Temple at Alexandria—started working with them energetically. This went on to bring up old memories, resolve outstanding issues, and heal the wounds of the past. Our shared lives in Israel and in Egypt were such times of high drama that they have left their imprint on many of our subsequent lives, right down to today.

Just think of what was involved here. The soul group which had been incarnating around Jeshua since the time of Atlantis had gathered for a big push forward into the Light. For a time it looked as if the Children of the Light, led by a great Teacher, would triumph and usher in a new era of Peace and Light. And then came the crucifixion—a deep trauma which has cast a long shadow right up to the present day.

But now the energy is changing and moving and taking the narrative to a new level. And what these books did was to move the story on for members of the Essene soul family by initiating a healing process. The energy of our Teacher came through and gently led us into a bigger understanding that we could let go of these energies now because only by doing that can we follow him into the Light of the new Consciousness. And through his eyes we began to see a different future for this soul family, these wonderful Workers in the Light who were and are our colleagues and friends. And as each individual healed, the healing spread and grew, and gradually we began to let go of our story and focus instead upon the energy of our Teacher and the energy of the Light which he represents.

And now as this last book in the sequence goes out into the world, the process of healing is moving into its final stages. And what is emerging is a clearer picture of the group as a whole. For, as members of the Essene soul family connected with us, we became aware that it was more like a family coming together than strangers coming in to do past-life sessions. So we send out our love to all the members of the soul family who have shared— and are sharing—this journey with us, for now as a group we are getting ready to step into a new future and a new beginning which the efforts of our two main Teachers, Jeshua and Mary Magdalene, have made possible.

37. A Time for Gathering

Alariel: The Essene Soul Family, the group of kindred spirits who incarnated with Jeshua in Israel 2,000 years ago, is now passing through a stage of Resolution and Reconnection. Many intense and heavy energies and much emotional pain has been coming up to be resolved and healed. That process of Resolution is well-advanced, and the soul family is now moving into a process of Reconnection.

This Essene soul family, which went on to be Gnostics, Franciscans, Cathars, and latterly Lightworkers became dispersed and scattered, but now it is time to reconnect mind to mind and heart to heart.

You can link up through the modern process of email with kindred spirits all over the world, and the old feeling of isolation is giving way to a new sense of coming together and sharing. That sharing is intensified whenever groups meet physically, either in their own country or on an international basis. This is why Essene Soul Family Gatherings are so important now, and why many people are focusing on them throughout the world. We urge you to reconnect in any way that seems appropriate to you at this special time.

Comment by Stuart: To facilitate this process of Reconnection, we have set up a network of international coordinators to cover all the countries in which we have readers (please see the Coordinators section at the end of this book.)

We encourage readers to set up their own groups and their own Gatherings. And we would appreciate it if you could tell the Coordinator for your country if you are having a Gathering or setting up a local group in your area. This will also help anyone who is traveling to link up with events happening in the destination country.

38. The Trilogy Emerges

In many ways, this book is the completion of a journey which began with our first book, *The Essenes: Children of the Light,* and continued through *Power of the Magdalene.* Here in the present book we reconnect with Essene past lives and then move on to look at the Gnostic movement and the greatest teacher working within that movement, Mary Magdalene.

Looking back, we can see how far we have come on this journey of discovery, a journey shared with many friends who have come to us in this quiet valley set in the heart of Devon, to explore their past lives. Here on this special site with ancient Druid links, we have opened the door on the Essene and Gnostic world that so many of us in this soul family share.

So much of the story of these books has been bound up with the past-life work we have done in this special place, and those who came in to do this work were often doing it not only for themselves but also to help in the healing process within the wider Essene Family. And so many people have reported the sense of grief at Jeshua's suffering and departure but also the great joy of being alive when this supreme Teacher walked the Earth to bring guidance, inspiration, and healing. To resonate with this shared experience has been part of the healing process of everyone who has traveled on this journey with us.

The revelations within this book of the depth and extent of Mary Magdalene's wisdom form a fitting conclusion to this drama. Nothing you may have read will have prepared you for the power of Mary's words contained in the Magdalene Summaries in this book. Here at last we have the opportunity to hear her in a way that has not been possible for 2,000 years. On the island of Cyprus Mary came into her own and found her real voice. When you read these Magdalene Summaries, it is just like being in the audience at those wonderful Midsummer Gatherings!

It was one of the hallmarks of the Essenes that they could work harmoniously together *as a team.* And we see an echo of that process in all the contributions to this series of books by readers who came up with interesting questions, as well as by all those who came in to do past-life work. Those past-life experiences—like those of Laura Clare and Akhira in *Power of the Magdalene* and Yianna, Lyn, and Sara in the present book—have provided real breakthroughs in understanding, and this has led to an increase in the energy of liberation and empowerment felt by many readers. It was as if the individuals were making breakthroughs not only for themselves but for the whole Essene Soul Family.

And so with the present volume, the Essene Trilogy now stands complete:

The Essenes: Children of the Light,
Power of the Magdalene, and
The Magdalene Version.

This Trilogy takes us from the foundation of the Essene communities through the dramatic times experienced by the disciples, especially the female disciples, and on into the Gnostic movement and the wisdom of Mary Magdalene. This book moves the story forward in ways which at the beginning of the writing process, we could not even begin to imagine. Even as late as August 2011, we were struggling to understand the powerful energetic nature of these books. During that month, we had two visits that helped to clarify this.

First, our friends, Bernadette Boutros and her sister Rima, visited us from Australia. They said that they see these books as a gateway, a way of accessing past-life experiences and connecting with Essene memories. In the case of many readers, this can lead to a process of activation and a sense of reconnecting with the Essene Soul Family.

Then later in August 2011, our friend Marina Sturm came from Austria. Marina is a teacher and workshop leader who has an acute awareness of the energies involved in the spiritual path, and, as she said, "If the process in your energy field is starting, then the book is your tool."

These friends helped us to see the energetic side of these books with greater clarity, and the many emails we receive from readers all over the world show us how much these books can open a door into that magical time when we sat at the feet of Jeshua and Mary Magdalene.

The one common theme in this Trilogy has been the fact that the Essenes worked as a big team so the Essene story is made up of many individual accounts contributing to the bigger picture. This Narrative runs parallel with the traditional account and features many of the same key characters, but it gives a very different perspective on the events of 2,000 years ago. The Essenes through their contacts with the Kaloo and the Order of Melchizedek knew many things that went far beyond the knowledge of the early Church Fathers. This deeper understanding of Jeshua, his life and his work, provides a much richer and more profound perspective on the events of that vital time. What this adds up to is a whole new alternative history to lay alongside the traditional account. That alternative history is gathering strength as each individual steps forward to tell his or her story, and this process is not over yet—in fact, it has only just begun.

39. Relationship Charts

A number of readers have asked us to produce a chart showing the extended family tree of the group around Jeshua, all the more necessary because the female disciples were a tightly-knit group with many family connections. We have prepared several charts to fill this need with the appropriate chapters in books of the Essene Trilogy being indicated by these abbreviations:

COL= *The Essenes, Children of the Light*
POM= *Power of the Magdalene*
MV= *The Magdalene Version*

For example, a reference reading *POM9* indicates Chapter 9 in the second book of the Essene Trilogy, *Power of the Magdalene.*

We will start with a chart illustrating the direct relationship links to Daniel, my persona in the first book; the abbreviation 'm' stands here for "married," and where the name is unknown, this is indicated with a question mark.

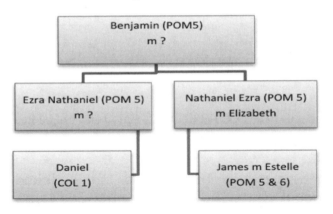

Now we can move on to a chart focusing on Joachim/Joseph:

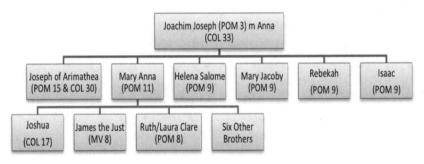

Next a chart showing Joseph's children by one of his marriages:

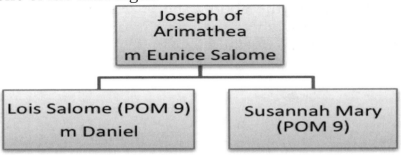

Finally a chart showing the relationships of Joseph of Arimathea's siblings:

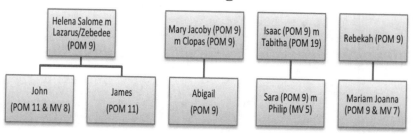

The whole extended family of Jeshua contains many of his disciples and spiritual followers and supporters. Chapter 10 in *Power of the Magdalene* which is called "An Angelic Conference" shows how this great team within the soul family was put together in the Interlife long before they came into incarnation upon the Earth.

Part Nine:

Conclusion

It is only with the heart
that one can see rightly;
what is essential
is invisible to the eye.

Antoine de Saint-Exupéry

40. The Continuing Journey

Comment by Stuart: This book also marks the end of a chapter in my personal journey. When in October 2010, Joanna and I visited Glastonbury to facilitate a past-life session for our friend Shelle Elizabeth, one significant gem of wisdom emerged from this process: "Allow the journey to be the journey."

That personal journey has focused for over twenty years on a beautiful, rambling old house in a quiet Devon valley where Joanna and I held our groups and explored so many past lives. And as I look back on these years, I remember all the good friends we have met along the way, and the many encounters with the wise Beings who inspired us. And from each of these encounters I learned something, and I also learned from writing these books, for every book is a journey in itself.

From my encounter with Mary Magdalene's energy—much more intense for me now than it was when I worked on *Power of the Magdalene*—I have learned so much, but one thing stands out above all else:

> The journey is not about words.
> It's about energy and process
> and love in the heart.

To me, this is the very core of what Mary Magdalene stood for, and she has helped me to see how deeply flawed our Western culture is and how much we need to move beyond a narrow intellectual approach. Yet I also learned something else from writing this book—I learned that knowledge is never entirely lost; it's simply waiting to be recovered. And what Alariel helped us to recover for this book is a strand of Truth that has not been accessible for 2,000 years.

I am so grateful to Alariel for his part in my journey. I realize now that I wouldn't have gotten very far without him, and to him and his whole angelic team, I send my deepest thanks. And now as I write these words to complete the final revisions on this book, Alariel is telling me that it is time for him to move on. He says his work with me is finished now as this Essene Trilogy was always going to be the central focus of our collaboration. And as he shuts down his channeling through me, he adds "Mission accomplished."

Here I echo the experience of many friends who are finding that the strands of their work are coming together now within a Holistic framework. In this book the theme of Oneness links the work of three great souls: Mary Magdalene 2,000 years ago, Sosan in the year 600, and Chief Seattle in the 1850s. Coming from three very different traditions, they share a vision of One Earth, One Universe, and One Humanity—a vision to lift us out of our divisive history and inspire us to explore the possibility of peace and unity at a time of Transition and Ascension.

41. The Song of Ascension

Where are the poets of the New World?
Where are those that sing
the reconnection with the soul,
the pioneers who point towards the goal
of life immortal
and the joy that never ends?

Who now explores what happens
when the Spirit blends
with the awakened heart?
Who sings the part
our many lives have played
in sweet illusion or in glory bright?

Who sings the journey
to the greater Light,
the swift expanding consciousness,
the flight of fear
and all the littleness that vies
to keep us earthbound
when we long to rise?

Who sings the brotherhood of angels
and of men?
Who sings the sisterhood of prophecy and
Light?
Who sings the soaring upwards
as we go beyond

the limitations that have held us all in bond?

Who sings the joy
when voyagers return at last
into the Light that is their Source
in which their very nature is revealed
when story dies,
and Truth trumps all the lies,
and all our hurts are healed?

Stuart Wilson

42. Epilogue:

On Faith in the Heart

The extract from the *Xin Xin Ming* in Chapter 30 covers only about a third of the original poem. To enable readers to see the scope and power of the full text, I give here the complete new version which I prepared for this book. This is a free version, not a word-for-word translation, and it has been made possible by the other translations listed in the Further Reading section.

The Way of Oneness

There is nothing difficult
about the Way of Oneness
when picking and choosing are set aside,
and all is accepted.
Once you stop longing and loathing,
everything becomes clear,
but make even the smallest preference,
and your whole world is divided.

If you wish to see the truth,
live with an open mind
and do not be for or against anything.
To swing between extremes of liking and disliking
is a sickness of the mind.

When the Way is not understood.
striving has no purpose.
Truth just *is,*
but the clouded mind can't see it.

The Way is vast and perfect like space;
it lacks nothing and has nothing in excess.
Silence the mind
and know this perfection.
It is through choosing and rejecting
that we miss the real nature of things.

Do not get entangled in the outer world
or lost in the inner emptiness;
stay serene in the Oneness of things
and duality vanishes by itself.

Trying to still the mind
only shifts the movement inward,
for then there is the mind
and you-in-motion-trying-to-still-it.
As long as you remain in the extremes
of movement and stillness,
you will not know Oneness.
When Oneness is not understood,
there is a double loss;
neither in the outer objects
nor in the inner emptiness
can the Real be found.

Believing that things are real,
you miss their true realness,
but believing that things are void and non-existent
also misses reality.
Live in the Way
where both ends of the equation

meet and become one,
where all paradoxes resolve themselves
in the transcendent Truth,
where action and stillness merge
and become one thing.

Talking and thinking
turn you from the harmony of the Way;
stop talking and thinking,
and you may experience Reality.
Awaken to Oneness to find its essence:
this goes beyond both emptiness and form.
In one moment of insight
we see beyond
both the outer surface and the inner emptiness.
Go beyond appearance and emptiness
and find the transcendent center.

The changes that seem to happen
in the outer world of form
are like the shadows of a dream.
They seem real because of our ignorance,
but it is simply shadow-play.
Do not go searching for the truth—
just throw away your opinions!

Avoid all aspects of duality—
they're illusions trying to deceive you again!
Confused by the extremes of duality,
it is easy to lose your way.
All dualities come from the One,
but do not cling to the One either!
If you do, there will be the One
and you-clinging-to-the-One!

When the heart is at peace with the Way,
nothing in the world offends—
no blame, no thing, no mind.
In the emptiness the mind is silent,
all false reality dissolves,
and the heart is unified and whole.
All the components of the universe
have returned to their origins,
and the many are again One.

Thinker and thought create each other—
look beyond both and see the One.
Don't look at the details
when you want to experience the One.
Because the mind can't describe Reality,
it cannot perceive it.
The heart is wiser
and simply knows the Real.
Oneness is neither hard nor easy;
it is beyond every opposite
because it contains and transcends them all.

To cling is to lose one's balance
open the hands, the mind, the heart,
and let it all go!
Let all be as it is:
flowing with the Way
you wander along,
free to be yourself.

Returning to your true nature,
you find the spontaneous essence
that holds everything.
If you walk the Way of Oneness
do not dislike any of it—
even the world of the senses.

For if you dislike anything at all,
there is that-thing and you-disliking-it.
Ah, duality again!
So accept it all
and do not dislike any of it.
Stop naming and describing things,
and rest in the silence of being.
In the emptiness of silent being,
you experience Reality as it is.

Cling to nothing and accept everything—
that is the path to the Light.
The wise do not strive for goals,
they stay unswayed and unattached.
The foolish weigh themselves down
with judging and choosing.

Awakened, there are no extremes
and no opposites—just a continuum of Oneness.
All the pairs of opposites are illusory dreams—
why try to grasp them?
Gain and loss, better and worse, greater and
lesser—throw them all out!

When we awaken, we see the Real,
not the dreams.
If the mind does not judge or choose,
then all things are as they are—
they are One.
Why look for troubles
when awareness of the One
frees you from all entanglements?

When the mind ceases to judge
and produce images,
you begin to see Reality

as a mystical whole.
Then the cool essence of being
pours into you,
and you return to your true nature.
Here rest and movement are one thing,
a transcendent reality
that cannot be described in words.
Here there is nothing to remember
and nothing to do.
All is empty, clear, and full of Light.

In the realm of the Real
there is neither self nor other;
awareness simply is.
To come into harmony with the Real,
just say, "Not Two."
When there is no duality,
all things are one and nothing can be separate;
the enlightened ones of all times and places
have entered into this truth.
This is an eternal state
and limits do not exist here.
Here there are no boundaries,
and comparisons are meaningless.

This state opens before your eyes
as a vast presence.

The dreams and comparisons and illusions
do not exist;
the seamless and undivided Real,
though invisible to most people,
is the true nature of things.

One Life in all beings,
all beings within one Web
of Consciousness and Life.
If this is understood, you are home already,
and there is no need to worry about being perfect.

When duality vanishes,
you enter true freedom.
Here words fail,
for this is a state beyond language.
In the Real there is no past, present, or future,
only the Eternal Now.

Note: The authorship of this classic Zen text has been disputed as it seems to contain references to later developments, so I asked Alariel for his comments on this.

Alariel: Because Sosan transcended time by integrating with Reality, he was able to anticipate future developments. That is why there are apparent anachronisms in the text that have led some scholars to assign a later date to it. Yet significantly, no one has come up with another credible name for the author. Common sense alone should make you question this: is it likely that this tradition—so careful and dedicated in so many ways—should have forgotten the name of the author of one of its greatest texts?

Further Reading

References to books on the Essenes are given in the Further Reading section of our first book, *The Essenes: Children of the Light,* so there is no need to repeat that information here. Only a few key books on Mary Magdalene are given here. A comprehensive listing of books on Mary appears on the website: www.findmarymagdalene.com

A bibliography listing the English translations of the *Xin Xin Ming* is given at the end of this section.

Astell, Christine. *Discovering Angels: Wisdom, Healing, Destiny.* Duncan Baird Publishers: London, 2005. A well-written, thorough, and beautifully illustrated introduction to the world of angels. (For workshops, see www.angellight.co.uk)

Bartlett, Dr. Richard. *Matrix Energetics: The Science and Art of Transformation.* Simon and Schuster: New York, NY, 2007. A remarkable and revolutionary book that applies the principles of quantum physics to the field of healing.

Bartlett, Dr. Richard. *The Physics of Miracles: Tapping into the Field of Consciousness Potential.* Simon and Schuster: New York, NY, 2009. How to apply the matrix forces known to physics in a personal process of transformation and empowerment. Highly recommended.

Braden, Gregg. *Awakening to Zero Point.* Radio Bookstore Press: Bellvue, WA, 1997. A helpful guide to the science underlying the transition of Earth and the change in consciousness.

Conze, Edward. *Further Buddhist Studies.* Bruno Cassirer: Oxford, 1975. Contains a remarkably insightful essay titled "Buddhism and Gnosis."

Cooper, Diana. *A New Light on Ascension.* Findhorn Press: Forres, Scotland, 2004. Written in a clear and direct style, this is much the best introduction to the whole field of ascension. Highly recommended.

de Boer, Esther. *The Gospel of Mary: Listening to the Beloved Disciple.* Continuum: London, 2005. Dr. de Boer is an established scholar who has published widely on Mary. Here she compares the portrayals of Mary in *The Gospel of Mary* and in the gospels of the New Testament.

Eckman, Jacelyn. *Veronica: The Lost Years of Jesus. 2010.* www.jacelyneckman.com The remarkable narrative of Veronica, a cousin of Jesus, sharing her memories of the travels and the ministry of Jesus and the parallel role of the women in his life. The first of a trilogy of books that are written in a way that brings these events to life. Highly recommended.

Gardner, Laurence. *The Magdalene Legacy.* Element: London, 2005. A beautifully written and thoroughly researched survey of all the main sources in Magdalene scholarship.

Gifford, Eli and Cook, Michael (Editors). *How Can One Sell the Air? Chief Seattle's Vision.* Book Publishing Company: Summertown, TN, 1992. Gives the full text of the Smith and Arrowsmith versions of the speech, together with Ted Perry's film script that was inspired by it.

Giusti, Debra. *Transforming Through 2012: Leading Perspectives on the New Global Paradigm.* Yinspire Media: CA, 2010. An insightful and balanced anthology of essays by thirty-three authors, including scientists, researchers, and futurists, as well as mystics and indigenous elders.

Heartsong, Claire and Clemett, Catherine Ann. *Anna, The Voice of the Magdalenes.* S.E.E. Publishing: www.claireheartsong.com, 2010. The eagerly-awaited sequel to *Anna, Grandmother of Jesus.* A book full of drama and direct insight into the lives of the greater family of Jesus.

Hurtak, James J. and Hurtak, Desiree. *Pistis Sophia: A Coptic Gnostic Text with Commentary.* The Academy for Future Science: Los Gatos, CA, 1999. Fascinating gnostic material from the Askew Codex, discovered in Egypt in 1773. This book is a remarkable gnostic dialogue on consciousness, Light, and the spirit of wisdom. Contains the full text with an insightful modern commentary.

Hurtak, James J. *Gnosticism: Mystery of Mysteries.* A Study in the Symbols of Transformation. The Academy for Future Science: Los Gatos, CA, 1999. A broad and scholarly overview of the whole area of Gnostic thought.

King, Karen L. *The Gospel of Mary of Magdala: Jesus and the First Woman Apostle.* Polebridge Press: Salem, Oregon, 2003. Includes a fine modern translation of *The Gospel of Mary.* A thoroughly readable account full of deep honesty that transforms scholarly material into inspiring communication.

Kirkel, Mercedes. *Mary Magdalene Beckons: Join the River of Love.* To be published in 2012. www.marymagdalenebeckons.com A clear, profound, and reliable transmission of the whole range of Mary Magdalene's practical teachings. If you want to hear the *real voice* of Mary Magdalene, we recommend that you buy this book.

Krishnamurti, Jiddu. *At the Feet of the Master.* Quest Books: Wheaton, IL. (The first edition was published in 1910 under the pen-name "Alcyone.") These are the words of the Master Koot Hoomi (a later incarnation of the apostle John) written down by his disciple. As a simple yet profound guide to the spiritual path, this little book has no equal.

Melchizedek, Drunvalo. *Living in the Heart: How to Enter into the Sacred Space within the Heart.* (Book and audio CD) Light Technology Publishing: Flagstaff, AZ 2003. A wonderfully wise and insightful book, combined with a beautifully produced meditation CD. Highly recommended.

Nahmad, Claire and Bailey, Margaret. *The Secret Teachings of Mary Magdalene.* Watkins: London, 2006. Includes the lost verses of *The Gospel of Mary,* revealed and published for the first time. A view of Mary perceived as the spiritual equal of Jesus, and her gospel revealed in its complete form through a channeling process.

O'Brien, Christian. *The Path of Light.* The Patrick Foundation: 1999. www.goldenageproject.org.uk An abridged free translation of two gnostic texts, the *Askew Codex* and the *Bruce Codex,* brought to England by James Bruce in 1769 and bequeathed to the Bodleian Library in Oxford. A remarkable book that reveals *The Path of Light* as a treatise on spiritual truths taught in the Druidic, Mystery and Brotherhood schools of the ancient world.

Pagels, Elaine. *The Gnostic Gospels.* Penguin Books: London, 1990. A scholarly but very readable account of gnostic material from the Nag Hammadi Library. This book has established itself as a key text within the whole area of gnostic scholarship.

Pagels, Elaine. *Beyond Belief: The Secret Gospel of Thomas.* Macmillan: London, 2003. A fascinating and clearly-written book that contrasts the rigidity of the Church with the flexibility and openness to innovation of the gnostic movement.

Picknett, Lynn. *Mary Magdalene: Christianity's Hidden Goddess.* Robinson: London, 2003. A controversial and fascinating book which describes Mary as a leading disciple and the wife of Jesus.

Prince, Sharon. *John of Old, John of New: The Awakening of an Apostle.* Shining Brightly Books: Houston, Texas, 2008 www.johnofnew.com The remarkable spiritual journey of John Davis, who discovers past-life experiences as the apostle John. A gripping story told in a direct and engaging way. Highly recommended.

Robinson, James (Editor). *The Nag Hammadi Library in English.* Harper Collins: San Francisco, 1990. The ultimate reference-book for many gnostic sources with complete translations of all the Nag Hammadi scrolls.

Starbird, Margaret. *The Goddess in the Gospels: Reclaiming the Sacred Feminine.* Bear and Co.: Rochester, VT, 1998. A profound and courageous book which re-examines the role of the sacred feminine in the early years of Christianity.

Wilson, Stuart and Prentis, Joanna. *Power of the Magdalene.* Ozark Mountain Publishing: Huntsville, AR, 2009. Based on the past-life experiences of seven subjects. This is our second book, containing a lot more information about the female disciples and the importance of Mary Magdalene as the spiritual partner of Jeshua. Also contains a section on the New Children, focusing especially on the Crystal Children.

Note: Some of the books cited above (especially the more esoteric titles) may be difficult to source from general bookshops. They can be obtained from these sources:

Arcturus Books, www.arcturusbooks.co.uk phone 01803 864363

Aristia, www.aristia.co.uk phone 01983 721060

Cygnus Books, www.cynus-books.co.uk phone 0845 456 1577

The eleven major English translations of the classic Zen text, *Xin Xin Ming* by Sosan follow in order of original publication.

Suzuki, Professor Daisetz Teitaro. *Manual of Zen Buddhism.* Grove Press: New York (original edition 1935). D.T. Suzuki also published a revised version with a number of small changes in *Buddhist Scriptures* edited by Edward Conze.

Waley, Arthur. *Buddhist Texts Through the Ages.* Oneworld Publications: Oxford, 1995. Original edition by Bruno Cassirer, Oxford, 1954.

Blyth, Reginald Horace. *Zen and Zen Classics: Selections from R.H. Blyth.* Compiled by Frederick Franck, Heian International: Torrance, CA, 1978. Original edition with more extensive commentaries by Hokuseido Press: Tokyo, 1960.

Yu, Upasaka Lu K'uan (Charles Luk). *Practical Buddhism.* Rider: London, 1971.

Clarke, Richard B. *Daily Chants.* Rochester Zen Center: New York, 1985. Available online at www.texaschapbookpress.com with parallel comparison of the Clarke and Suzuki translations. See also Rochester Zen Center's *Chants and Recitations* noted later in these references.

Sheng-Yen, Master. *Faith in Mind: A Guide to Ch'an Practice.* Dharma Drum Publications: Elmhurst, NY, 1987. At the time of this publication, available online at www.terebess.hu/english/hsin3

Pajin, Professor Dusan. "On Faith in Mind," *Journal of Oriental Studies*, Volume xxvi, no 2. Hong Kong, 1988. At the time of this publication, available online at www.sacred-texts.com/bud/zen

Myokyo-ni, The Venerable (Irmgard Schloegl). *The Middle Way*. The Buddhist Society: London, May 1999.

Dunn, Philip and Jourdan, Peter. *The Book of Nothing: A Song of Enlightenment*. Andrews McMeel: Kansas City, 2002.

Rochester Zen Center. *Chants and Recitations*. Rochester Zen Center: Rochester, New York, 2005. This is the Richard B. Clarke translation, extensively modified by members of the Rochester Zen Center.

Ho, Lok Sang. (Undated.) At the time of this publication, available online at www.In.edu.hk/econ/staff/Xin%20Xin%20Ming.doc Click on link. View as HTML.

Acknowledgments

We would like to say a big thank you to those whose past-life experiences form an essential part of this book:

Jaye Woodfield

Lyn

Pam

Our thanks to Paul Tamplin for help with our computers and for setting up our website so brilliantly.

Our thanks to Catherine Mary La Toure for her friendship and support. The meetings Stuart had with her in 2009 were a key to turning his thoughts towards *The Gospel of Mary* and the possibility of going beyond that text and recovering Mary Magdalene's inner teachings. Cathie's website lists the full range of books on Mary Magdalene, and it can be visited at www.findmarymagdalene.com. We must also mention her Magdalene Flowers Spray called "The Magdalene Gift," which proved most helpful in assisting Stuart in tuning in to Mary's energy as part of the channeling process. Thank you, Cathie! Catherine Mary would be delighted if those who feel they have an active part to play in tracing the Magdalene's journey through France would like to contact her by email through her website.

Our thanks to Anne MacEwen, President of the Essene Network International, and to Sylvia

Moss and Chrissie Astell for their continuing friendship and support. ENI's website is www.essenenetwork.org

Towards the end of August 2010, our friend Janie rang us with news of a remarkable N.L.P. session that contributed a new layer of understanding to this book. Thank you, Janie, and a big thank you also to Emma, who facilitated the session.

In October 2010, we went to Glastonbury to facilitate a past-life session for our friend, Shelle Elizabeth. During that session, the words quoted in the final chapter emerged. At that time we also met Shelle's friend Anya Kumara, an Initiated Magdalene Priestess. It was a wonderful day! Our thanks to both of you!

Our thanks to all our International Coordinators: their work helps to bring the Essene Soul Family together. And many thanks to William Brune of Missouri for facilitating our Yahoo group, which can be accessed through essene_family. Our thanks also to William for his email dialogue involving Alariel from which the term "Rainbow Tapestry of Truth" emerged.

A big *thank you* to the whole Ozark Mountain Publishing team, especially Dolores Cannon, Julia Degan, Nancy Garrison, Joy Newman and Itera Clehouse. Thank you for helping us to get these new perspectives out into the world. During the editing process, Dolores encouraged us to extend the text. This resulted in the two question and answer chapters. Thank you, Dolores, for your vital contribution!

The Essene Gathering near Lyme Regis in Dorset in March 2011 that was hosted by our friends Lyn and Graham brought a time of high energy and deep connection with kindred spirits. Our thanks to Lyn and Graham and to our main speaker at the Gathering, Sharon Prince, for focalizing the love and energy of Mary Magdalene so powerfully. (Sharon's website is www.sharonprince.net)

Our thanks to Josee Honeyball for her major contribution to Chapter 9. Watching her facilitate a Matrix Energetics session for Joanna at the time of the Gathering opened up a whole new line of enquiry. (Josee's website is www.heartfieldalchemy.com)

One of our great discoveries at the Gathering were the books of Jacelyn Eckman. Her memories of Veronica, a cousin of Jesus, are a wonderful and powerful account of life at that time. Thank you, Jacelyn! (Jacelyn's website is www.jacelyneckman.com)

We are most grateful to Mercedes Kirkel for sharing her book, *Mary Magdalene Beckons: Join the River of Love* with us at the manuscript stage. The text encouraged us by showing that others were receiving parallel information. Thank you, Mercedes!

Our thanks to Professor Ted Perry for permission to use quotations from his film script within the context of my version of Chief Seattle's speech. This version attempts to bring the energy of the speech fully into line with current issues and concerns.

Our thanks go to Pete Stickland for his major contribution to Chapter 23. As part of a past-life session, Pete was able to access a higher level of consciousness and bring through a key statement of Mary Magdalene's wisdom.

Our thanks extend to Cecily of the Rochester Zen Center for providing sources and information.

Our thanks go to Bernadette Boutros and her sister Rima from Australia for sharing their insights on the Essene energies and to Marina Sturm who came from Austria and talked to us about the energies in the books. Your visits in August 2011 brought many blessings!

Comment by Stuart: And finally, I must express my deep gratitude to my teachers during past-life experiences in Zen monasteries. Without their help, I would never have been able to prepare a new version of the *Xin Xin Ming*.

Index

About the Authors

Joanna Prentis: I was born in Bangalore in southern India. When I was nearly three, my family returned to Scotland where I spent my childhood and teenage years. After leaving school, I traveled extensively, married and lived in Hong Kong for two years and then ten years in the bush in Western Australia, where my three daughters were born. It was there that my interest began in alternative medicine and education, organic farming, metaphysics and meditation. With a local nurse, we ran a Homeopathic and Radionic practice.

I returned to the UK in 1979 and later trained as a Montessori teacher, educating my two youngest daughters, Katinka and Larissa, at home for a few years. I now have four beautiful grandchildren.

I have certificates in various healing modalities and hold a foundation diploma in Humanistic Psychology. I also trained with Ursula Markham and have a diploma in Hypnotherapy and Past Life Therapy.

With my eldest daughter Tatanya, I set up the Starlight Centre in 1988, a centre for healing and the expansion of consciousness. Over the years, Tatanya has introduced us to many innovative techniques and interesting people.

In 1999 we closed the Centre to focus on producing our books. I continue with my Past Life work, and readers now connect with us from all over the world.

You can visit Joanna at her website:
www.foundationforcrystalchildren.com

Stuart with Joanna Printis, his co-author on the Essene Trilogy.

COPYRIGHT WYN PENNANT JONES PHOTOGRAPHIC ART

Stuart Wilson is a writer on new perspectives. His perceptions have been developed through 30 years of working with groups committed to personal growth. For nine years, Stuart co-focalized (with Joanna Prentis) the Starlight Centre in the West of England, a centre dedicated to healing and the transformation of consciousness.

He writes about this period:

"It was inspiring and fascinating but also exhausting! A stream of visitors came in to the Centre, mainly from the United States and Australia, but some also from Europe. We had an amazing and mind-bending time sitting at the feet of internationally respected spiritual teachers and workshop leaders."

Part of the work of the Centre was research into past lives, and this led to his collaboration with Joanna to write *The Essenes, Children of the Light* and *Power of the Magdalene*, both published by Ozark Mountain Publishing

You can visit Stuart at his website:
www.foundationforcrystalchildren.com

Feedback from Readers

Please let us know how you feel about this book. You can contact us through our website: www.foundationforcrystalchildren.com

We are sometimes asked by readers when the next Starlight Centre meeting will be. Although the Starlight Centre doesn't meet physically anymore, we do "meet" on our website and through our growing correspondence with readers all over the world. We also have a Yahoo group that we invite you to join. You can find it under essene_family. And if you're visiting the West of England and want to come and see us, please email because we both have busy schedules.

Comment by Stuart:

When we reached the final stage of revisions on the manuscript of this book, Alariel shut down his channeling through me with the words "Mission accomplished." I send my deepest thanks to him and his angelic team for all their help during the production of the Essene Trilogy. None of this would have been possible without their help.

International Coordinators

One theme that has emerged strongly from many of the emails we get from readers is a feeling of isolation, of being surrounded by conventional people with a different value system and a materialistic way of life. This feeling very often leads to a need to contact and talk with like-minded people.

So many readers have asked us for contacts that we have set up a network of International Coordinators, one for each country (or group of countries) where we have readers. If you would like to contact other people in your area or in another country, please email your local Coordinator with your email address and the name of your country and nearest city. The Coordinator will then give you email addresses of any local readers who are on his/her list.

So far we have Coordinators in the following countries:

United Kingdom: Lyn and Graham Whiteman
        at essenes@btinternet.com
USA: Diane Richard at diane@biosophic.com
Canada: Mary Pat Fuchs at mpfessene@gmail.com
Australia: Jann Porter at rosepath@iprimus.com.au
Ireland: Christine Astell at c.angels@btinternet.com
Germany and.Atistria: Norbert and Karin Karin -
        at bauschat.karin@web.de
        Norbert at beine.norbert@web.de
Portugal: Martin Northey at martin.northey@mail.telepac.pt
Spain: Isabel Zaplana at i.zaplana@gematria.net
France: to be agreed
Scandinavia: Anita Murray at anita.murray@ymail.com
Central Europe: To be agreed
Africa: Pieter van Nieuwenhuizen at Pieter@sotiralis.co.za
Bermuda: Mimi Harding at moomimi@logic.bm
Southeast Asia: To be agreed

If you would like to be a Coordinator for any country without a Coordinator or not listed, please contact us via our website—see the Feedback from Readers section.

The New Media

Many people are now exploring new levels of empowerment through using the new media, particularly social media and internet radio.

Social media link people in immediate and personal ways, supporting the democratization of knowledge and empowering individuals whatever the political environment.

Internet radio empowers Lightworkers by providing a vital resource of information on new ideas and the New Consciousness.

The importance of internet radio stations as a vital resource in a time of change is now being more widely recognized. The most effective format here is the one-hour weekly show in which the host can dialogue with guests who have interesting ideas to share about the changes that are happening in our lives. Add the efficiency of international phone cables connecting host with guests through optical fibre technology so that the host can be in America and the guests in UK, or Europe, or Australia, and you get a glimpse of the truly global nature of internet radio.

Listening live to these shows is only part of their appeal. There is also an archive of past shows which is a real treasure house of alternative information. Leading internet radio stations that offer a progressive and alternative view of the world include:
www.bbsradio.com
www.radiooutthere.com
www.soulsjourneyradio.com
www.talkshoe.com
www.worldpuja.org

Other Books by

Stuart Wilson and Joanna Prentis

The Essenes, Children of the Light

The inner story of the Essene Brotherhood, seen from the past life perspective of Daniel, an Essene elder, and his friend Joseph of Arimathea. Tells the dramatic story of Jesus' healing in the tomb and reveals Essene links with the Druids and the Order of Melchizedek.

Power of the Magdalene

A blend of the past life experiences of seven subjects and channeling by Alariel. Reveals the existence of a group of female disciples, and the real significance of Mary Magdalene as the spiritual partner of Jeshua. Contains a whole section on the New Children who are now being born.

Atlantis and the New Consciousness

A journey of exploration into the world of Atlantis, a time of amazing technology, deep healing, and profound wisdom. Based upon channeling and past-life experiences and revealing much entirely new information about Atlantis.

Beyond Limitations: The Power of Conscious Co-Creation

Channeled information from the angelic source Alariel which provides a complete answer to the question, "How do we create our own reality?" A revolutionary text which reveals the connection between reality creation and the 2012 experience. This is quite simply the most advanced book on reality creation available anywhere.

Other Books Published
by
Ozark Mountain Publishing, Inc.

Conversations with Nostradamus, Volume I, II, III.................by Dolores Cannon
Jesus and the Essenes...by Dolores Cannon
They Walked with Jesus..by Dolores Cannon
Between Death and Life.. by Dolores Cannon
A Soul Remembers Hiroshima...by Dolores Cannon
Keepers of the Garden...by Dolores Cannon
The Legend of Starcrash..by Dolores Cannon
The Custodians...by Dolores Cannon
The Convoluted Universe - Book One, Two, Three, Four......by Dolores Cannon
Five Lives Remembered ....by Dolores Cannon
The Three Waves of Volunteers and the New Earth .... by Dolores Cannon
I Have Lived Before..by Sture Lönnerstrand
The Forgotten Woman...by Arun & Sunanda Gandhi
Luck Doesn't Happen by Chance....................................by Claire Doyle Beland
Mankind - Child of the Stars............................by Max H. Flindt & Otto Binder
Past Life Memories As A Confederate Soldier.........................by James H. Kent
Holiday in Heaven...by Aron Abrahamsen
Out of the Archives .... by Aron & Doris Abrahamsen
Is Jehovah An E.T.?..by Dorothy Leon
The Essenes - Children of the Light...............by Stuart Wilson & Joanna Prentis
Power of the Magdalene...............................by Stuart Wilson & Joanna Prentis
Beyond Limitations ....by Stuart Wilson & Joanna Prentis
Atlantis and the New Consciousness .... by Stuart Wilson & Joanna Prentis
Rebirth of the Oracle.................................by Justine Alessi & M. E. McMillan
Reincarnation: The View from Eternity......by O.T. Bonnett, M.D. & Greg Satre
The Divinity Factor..by Donald L. Hicks
What I Learned After Medical School ....by O.T. Bonnett, M.D.
Why Healing Happens..by O.T. Bonnett, M.D.
A Journey Into Being..by Christine Ramos, RN
Discover The Universe Within You..by Mary Letorney
Worlds Beyond Death..by Rev. Grant H. Pealer
A Funny Thing Happened on the Way to Heaven .... by Rev. Grant H. Pealer
Let's Get Natural With Herbs...by Debra Rayburn
The Enchanted Garden...by Jodi Felice
My Teachers Wear Fur Coats........................by Susan Mack & Natalia Krawetz
Seeing True...by Ronald Chapman
Elder Gods of Antiquity..by M. Don Schorn
Legacy of the Elder Gods..by M. Don Schorn
Gardens of the Elder Gods .... by M. Don Schorn
Reincarnation...Stepping Stones of Life ....by M. Don Schorn

Continue for more books by Ozark Mountain Publishing, Inc.

For more information about any of the above titles, soon to be released titles, or
other items in our catalog, write or visit our website:

OZARK
MOUNTAIN
PUBLISHING

PO Box 754
Huntsville, AR 72740
www.ozarkmt.com
1-800-935-0045/479-738-2348
Wholesale Inquiries Welcome